Success
is
You

Henry E. Ford

KENDALL/HUNT PUBLISHING COMPANY
4050 Westmark Drive Dubuque, Iowa 52002

"Mainly, I'm telling it because it may help someone else. Many a day I needed help, needed encouragement, needed to know that somebody else before me had walked this same road and was able to make it. Whatever the adversities may be, don't be fooled by them or think that's the way life will always be."

- Eula McClaney -

Ford & Associates
P.O. Box 393
Twinsburg, OH 44087-0393
(216) 348-4612

Cover Design by
Dorothy Hudson
Cleveland, Ohio

Cover Artwork by
Ameenah Shafeeq
Cleveland, Ohio

Foreword by
Margaret Ford-Taylor
Director of Karamu House, Inc.
Cleveland, Ohio

Edited by
Jean Ford-May
Vice President, Human Resources
College of Art and Design
Pasadena, California

> *"The more you surround yourself
> with the presence of greatness,
> the more difficult and unreasonable
> it becomes to fail."*
>
> Henry Ford

*"When you knock on opportunity's door,
make sure your bags are packed."*

- Dennis Green, NFL Head Coach -

*"It's not the load that breaks you down,
it's the way you carry it."*

- Lena Horne -

*"Don't be afraid to go out on a limb.
That's where the fruit is."*

- Janie Mines, first African-American graduate
from the U.S. Naval Academy -

*"Success doesn't mean the absence of failure;
it means the attainment of objectives."*

- Roy Roberts, corporate executive, General Motors -

Dedication

To The Memory of
My Mother and Father

To my mother and father, I owe the most. From them I received the sound principles which I place above profit and pleasure.

They taught me a sense of fairness and responsibility that has been my guiding light in a world too often filled with darkness. From that sense of fairness and responsibility I have developed a deep respect and concern for my fellow human beings.

Because of what my parents taught, I have developed nurturing relationships with family and friends. Those relationships are the basis for my direction and continued growth.

My parents taught me to try to look at the good side of everything. From them, I learned that during those times when life knocks me down and steps on me, I have two choices. I can be bitter because I'm down, or I can be thankful to be alive, feel the pain, and begin my way toward recovery.

They taught me to believe, so that even if everyone around me loses faith, I still have the capacity to say *"It's not over, until I give up."*

My mother and father's teachings have become the foundation of a house united. It is a house with walls that can withstand the bitterness of temporary defeat. It is a house with a roof that will provide shelter in the time of storm.

My house has served as a place of solitude when I felt all was against me. My house has been the command center from which I have battled loneliness and heartache. From my house I have experienced discrimination and defeat.

My house also has served as an oasis of hope in a desert of hopelessness. What I've learned in my house has given me a commitment to family. What I've learned in my house has allowed me to become that person which attracted my wife Dianne. What I've learned in my house has encouraged me to be that person who enjoys the respect of the winners in life.

To my father I owe thanks for the roof he placed over my head and the food he placed on the table. To him I owe thanks for teaching me to have a warm heart toward others. To him I owe thanks for teaching me to have a cool head in the midst of heated tempers or trying circumstances. He did not let a limited education become a stumbling block. He refused to let the lowly expectations of others set his upper limit. He set a standard that I hope someday to achieve.

To my mother I owe thanks for being both parents after the death of my father. It was she who managed to smile when there were plenty of reasons to cry. She shielded me while she was here and prepared me for the time when she would be gone. She was strong when illness told her to be weak. My mother set the standard for persistence which I speak of in the following pages.

If I could say nothing good about my parents but that they gave me life, that would be enough to allow for a brighter tomorrow. But they gave me much more, and that is why I consider myself to have been chosen to be a bright light in an often dark world.

Contents

Foreword

*"I am black **BUT** comely . . . "* Song of Solomon, I; 5.
*"I am black **AND** comely . . . "* Egyptian translation of the same
text. Look at the two totally different meanings given to the
passage through the two conjunctions *"BUT"* and *"AND."* The
"BUT" translation is defensive and acknowledges inferiority; the
"comely" hopefully and apologetically offered to lessen the
negativism of being black. The *"AND"* translation gives equal
value to both words, the *"black"* being as much of an asset as
"comely." The *"AND"* is an acknowledgment of equal worth in
both words. Now think of the millions of people who have been
negatively affected and the centuries of misery perpetuated
through the acceptance of one three-letter word - BUT.

This is a microcosm of how we as individuals, regardless
of color, are often manipulated consciously and unconsciously
into self-analysis that results in damaging and damning
psychological consequences. We have been told, or shown, in
so many ways that we are inferior or deficient, that we accept it.
Acceptance is easy since we are most often told or shown in
ways too subtle for easy detection and, most significantly, by
those entrusted with the development of our psyche. Often
through loving ignorance, parents, teachers and other primary
care providers subscribe, albeit unknowingly, to the larger evil
perpetuated by irresponsible historians and media makers as well
as those who have given over their souls to the making of
money.

What the following text does is to invite - implore - you
to RECOGNIZE whatever distortions you have come to accept
about yourself and to REALIZE that they are true only as long
as you accept them as truths. The author of this wonderful and
inspiring text took that journey and through the process of
recognizing and realizing, found that the possibilities in his life
were limitless. He discovered that he could and should be the

master of his own destiny.   It is a thrilling discovery and somewhat frightening. As stifling as the present environment is, it has grown comfortable for many of us.   To move out and upward takes great courage, often against seemingly insurmountable obstacles.   This text constantly calls upon the reader to return to the reaffirmation of self.   The self that you will decide to create and let unfold.

Sadly, most people will continue on from birth to grave in some state of frustrated non-fulfillment. Henry Ford encourages you not to be one of those people. He shares with you the truths of his discoveries and gives you the tools to RECOGNIZE and REALIZE your own potential. Finally, he invites you, through the courage of his own convictions, to take those first meaningful steps toward self-actualization and your true destiny which was God-given at birth.

Margaret Ford-Taylor
Director
Karamu House, Inc.

Preface

This book is about the challenge of making the most of what we have and becoming the best that we can become. The effects of wasted human potential defy quantitative description.

All that we seek to become and all that we fail to become is rooted in what we believe. All that the world lacks is traceable to those with the capacity to love, but the tendency to hate; to those with the resources to give, but the mindset to take; to those who can, but think they can't; to those who would have, but didn't; or to those who are planning to, but won't.

From what might appear to be an insignificant dream can sprout forth the cure for a dreaded disease or the solution for peace on earth. How different might the world be today had it not been for the persistence of Thomas Edison or Dr. Jonas Salk? How different might the lives of 30 million African Americans been, had it not been for the belief and commitment of Dr. Martin Luther King, Jr.?

Present in each of us is unrealized potential that all of us could benefit from. Life as we know it sometimes convinces us that it is better to be safe than successful.

Even if your dream doesn't become earth shattering, it can still become mind boggling. If it only changes *your* life, it should be worth it to you. How will you know how big your dream can be, unless you wake up and put it into action?

Success Is You is about creating your own recipe of greatness from the ingredients of education, attitude, belief and persistence. Over thirty years within corporate America provides the basis for the solid business perspective contained within this book.

Success Is You will take you from society's low expectations for the black male to the author's credible achievements. The book will help you understand how the author turned an aptitude for failure into an attitude for success.

Learn how to minimize racial and religious and other interpersonal tension by focusing on the positive. The author will describe ways that he turned the racial insensitivity of others into one of his greatest assets.

After reading **_Success Is You_**, you will be amazed at the power of obtaining a college degree, **_after_** the age of fifty. You will be amazed at the pieces that connected because of a career change, again **_after_** the age of fifty. The readers of this book can expect to be encouraged, led and challenged to take a more active role in bettering their lives. They will be led into situations of adversity, and given the author's response to the situation. The readers will become aware of examples of individuals who overcame adversity and found rewards at the end of that adversity.

In some cases, these people are well known in their fields of endeavor, they are the winners in life. The readers will be asked to search within themselves for evidence of latent desire, talent and ability. The readers will be given alternatives to the crippling effects of apathy and defeatism.

Acknowledgements

Borrowing from the old African proverb *"It takes a village to raise a child,"* I humbly submit that it takes *more* than a village to write a book.

Thanks first to my wife Dianne who has encouraged me to overcome adversity and doubt. She takes the smallest of my accomplishments and builds them up until I have no other choice but to be a success.

Thanks to my younger sister Jean for her invaluable help in editing this book and for being a role model. Thanks to my brother Aaron who I can always count on.

Thanks to Sherbia Jones, Ruth Mitchell and Ann Hoyle for arranging my first major speaking engagement. It was primarily that engagement which set the wheels in motion, making my speaking career and this book possible.

Thanks to Dr. Robert Lawson for introducing me to Kendall-Hunt Publishing Company, and for the kind words of encouragement. Thanks to Les Brown for taking the time to put my speaking career into overdrive.

Thanks to Bertram Gardner who has served as a mentor for over thirty years. Thanks for over thirty years of guiding me around the pitfalls and over the obstacles.

Thanks to Sherryl Burton, Shirley Craft, Leonard Hardy, Ben and Betty Suber, Katie Wilson and others who over the years have reviewed material that went into this book.

Thanks to Joe and June Taylor for helping boost my speaking engagements in the Cleveland area. Thanks to Robert and Anne Chapman for their interest in and ideas for the work I am doing. Thanks to Ors Banhidy whose computer wizardry made it possible for me to produce this book as a camera ready document.

Thanks to many friends and relatives whose interest and support have helped me to come this far, and laid the groundwork for me to go even further.

Introduction

Deeply rooted in the challenges we face on a daily basis are the seeds of personal failures, planted, fed and harvested by our own misconceptions. The libraries and book stores of this nation are filled with solutions to major organizational problems which are primarily traceable to individual problems. It is little wonder that we find it difficult to work with others, when we cannot work with ourselves.

Our *perceived* personal limitations, our fears and our prejudices combine to create a wall between ourselves and our personal greatness. We are the volunteer victims of our failed belief system.

Many times our solution to inequality manifests itself in bringing the subject of our disillusionment down to our level. Not often enough do we take the position that we want to climb to the top. I am reminded of the story of a jealous individual who complained that another worker received a larger raise. When asked what should be done about the situation, in a jealous rage the employee shouted *"take back the raise!"*

It never occurred to the employee that he should try to substantiate why he should have a larger raise. His position was to create a system of equal suffering instead of working toward a system of equal rewards. It's easier to tear down than to build but, I would add, a lot less productive.

Success Is You combines the foundation of education, experience and reflection. The purpose of **_Success Is You_** is to encourage you to create your own personal greatness. It will be a greatness that is not dependent upon the approval of others.

You will cease to be that person who is at the mercy of negative situations. You will begin to create your own positive situations. Once you realize the power you have to control your own destiny, you will understand that you have awakened a sleeping giant.

Welcome to **_Success Is YOU!_**

About *Success Is You*
Reader's Comments

"I wholeheartedly approve of publication of the proposed text which you submitted to me. It is informative and very well written. You have captured the essence of 'Karamu'..."

Margaret Ford-Taylor, Executive Director
Karamu House of Greater Cleveland

"Sense of direction is good."

Bertram Gardner
Former Community Relations Director
City of Cleveland

"I enjoyed it, it captures the essence of what we're about."

Marcia Mockabee, Mentor Coordinator
Career Beginnings Program at
Case Western Reserve University

"I am pleased you have selected me to be a part of what may become a best seller."

Kenneth L. Wilson, President
WILCO Information Management

- Section 1 -
Laying The Foundation

To Maya Angelou
A Response to *Today, The Rock Cries Out*

From Generation To Generation
To Larry, Shirletha, Tina. . .and Others

Definition, History and Study

Spreading The Message
My Opening Remarks to The 16th Annual Conference
of The Black Data Processing Associates

To Maya Angelou
A Response to *Today, The Rock Cries Out*

Thank you Maya Angelou, for surely you have spoken to us all. *Today, The Rock Cries Out* speaks phrases where mere words will not do, it seeks healing from wounds thought to be fatal, it finds truth in the midst of lies, it asks for forgiveness in the midst of oppression, it looks for pleasure in the midst of pain.

It reminds us that our permanence may be temporary, that our dominance may be illusory. It reminds us of our ignorance, our apathy, our misdeeds. It reminds us of our abuse and misuse of our planet.

Today, The Rock Cries Out reminds us that even in our diversity, we are one. It reminds us that whatever our origin, our race, our belief, that we all live by *The Rock, The River and The Tree.*

Today, The Rock Cries Out tells us that whatever history has done to us, whatever has been our pain and our misery, we stand today at a new frontier. It tells us that the knowledge of the past must become the building blocks of the future.

Today, The Rock Cries Out challenges us to a call for action. It places the blame on no one, but the responsibility on everyone. It calls upon us to reject our fears and to seek our greatness, to look to *The Rock, The River and The Tree.* It calls upon us to recognize the existence of a new day, made brighter by the painful lessons of yesterday.

Today, The Rock Cries Out brings us wisdom as old as the Scriptures and as basic as The Golden Rule. If we should choose to ignore its simple but eloquent message, like the dinosaur we may be off toward our hastening doom.

But let us hope that we will follow your urgings, and then perhaps humankind may indeed find a permanent place beside *The Rock, The River and The Tree.*

From Generation to Generation
To Larry, Shirletha, Tina. . .and Others

"You can be a bright light in an often dark world, if only you will believe and seek to achieve."

These words are to *All My Children* - - to Larry, Shirletha and Tina - - adults now, but still of great importance to me.   These words are also meant for others of the *twenty-something* generation.   There is a message from many of my generation that feels and speaks of our hopes and fears for those to whom we will pass the torch.

As you read the remainder of this book, you need to know of my commitment to the belief and principles that I describe.   You need to know that I am visionary to the point of attracting the disbelief of many.   As I move from vision to reality, I find the situation changing.   As I achieve my goals, I find doubters becoming extinct at a rapid rate.

My vision is to spread a positive influence to the far corners of the world.   My vision is to create a legacy that lives beyond my years on earth.   The beginning of such a formidable task begins at home.

I have made an investment in my future by being who I am.   I spent years being involved in service organizations, where I learned the needs and abilities of others.   For years I have been on the forefront of change.   I became an entrepreneur, while others questioned why I would do so when I had a *'secure'* job.   All these things are beginning to pay off.   I dared to be different and because I did, I am beginning to reap the rewards.

Part of my investment has been at a cost to you.   Part of the time I studied, we could have played.   Part of the time I was not there, I was engaged elsewhere in something of a positive nature.   I don't know whether I should apologize for not being there, or hope that you will just understand that I was pursuing my dream.

For what you sacrificed, I cannot repay.   I can only hope that what I have done will provide for you the inspiration to pursue your dreams.

It is you, the hope of tomorrow, that will be among the first to share the contents of this book. We are of two generations, separated not only by the uniqueness of our experiences, but by the effects of a rapidly changing world.

Mine is the generation that was born into a world without television. Yours is the generation that followed the first space walks. Mine is the generation that grew up in single telephone homes with one car garages. Yours is the generation of car phones, with several televisions in one home.

Mine is the generation that was openly denied freedom and equality with signs stating *"For Whites Only."* Yours is the generation of *"equal opportunity."* With that opportunity comes possibilities, not probabilities. For twentieth century America has new forms of slavery including complacency, drugs and self hate.

You must make that opportunity a reality by crystallizing your goals and focusing on your dreams. Part of your challenge will be to turn the clock forward on technological change. I hope that you will also take up the task of turning the clock back on moral values.

I mention that because mine is the generation where neighbors talked for hours over the back fence. Yours is the generation that finds neighbors not knowing each other. Mine is the generation that could not walk safely on the moon. Yours is the generation that cannot walk safely through our neighborhoods.

My challenge to your generation is to be on the cutting edge of change. My challenge to you is that you become a contributor to a rapidly changing world instead of a victim of it. You sometimes will have to take an unpopular stand. Sometimes you will be looked upon as being different, and you will be different.

You will be different like Jackie Robinson, you will be different like Andrew Young, you will be different like Nelson Mandela, you will be different like Mother Teresa, you will be different like Susan B. Anthony and Susan L. Taylor. Like others who realize and develop their potential, you will be counted among the winners in life. Remember that it can be lonely at the top, but it's also rewarding.

Although much has changed, I hope this book will convince you that there is more that binds us than that which separates us. The issues of education and involvement and support and respect and a love for each other and a love of self and a love of God are things that are not dated and time-stamped.

Our common vision, I would hope, would be a drug-free and crime-free society, one in which opportunity is color blind and gender blind. A society where all men and women are not only allowed, but encouraged to live out the true meaning of that higher power who created them.

To the extent that the vision is unrealized, your task is clear. You have the power and the purpose to contribute to the solutions, while working through the challenges. You can be a bright light in an often dark world, if only you will believe and seek to achieve.

God made no greater minds, and no kinder hearts than what you possess. With all that has been sacrificed by all the generations preceding and including your own, do not let evil, nor greed, nor apathy, nor lack of belief, nor lack of self respect, deny you your rightful place in history.

I have concluded that with our five senses, we are extensions of a power greater than our own. What we do with that power truly will have a profound effect on ourselves and all those we influence.

What I have done and will continue to do is offered to you on the following pages. I offer it with unconditional love, and with the hope that it helps you to achieve that which is important to you.

Definition, Study, History

"With thanks to Gould and others who seek truth beyond the walls of separation and with apologies to no one, I bring you conclusive evidence that Success Is YOU!

SUCCESS as defined by my Professional Write Software, lists accomplishment as the first of fourteen synonyms. There is a wide latitude of freedom to define success as you would like it to be. The word **YOU** has no synonyms listed for an obvious reason. The reason is that there is no substitute for **YOU**. So with the freedom to define success goes the obligation for you to be personally responsible for it. Success is non-transferable, it cannot be bought, sold, given or stolen. **Success simply and undeniably is YOU.**

Success Is You deals with attitude, education, training, motivation and persistence. Since the beginning of time, experts and lay people alike have discussed and debated the needs, causes and effects of these areas. The works of William James, Dale Carnegie and Zig Ziglar are recent proponents of a vast and diverse field of study. The task of helping us attain higher levels of achievement has been shared throughout history by teachers, ministers, parents, friends and anyone else who touches our lives in a positive manner.

Popular motivational speaker Les Brown, by his own words *"born in a shack and judged educable mentally retarded,"* has no formal education past the twelfth grade. He has become a multi-millionaire by becoming self taught, and by raising the hopes and aspirations of many followers. Many others bring numerous and impressive credentials to convince people of their inherent capacity to succeed.

Messengers of hope have come in many forms, bearing many messages, and yet there is much work to be done. What has been done will not likely be quantified or qualified in this or any other book. Having stated that, let me continue.

The methods of study I used began with observing those around me. For a long time, I have been intellectually inquisitive. For example, I wanted to know how the stock market worked, while those around me were intimidated by lack of current knowledge. I wanted to know why the banker looked more successful than I, and yet he or she used my money.

While others implied that what they didn't know, they couldn't learn, I rejected those conclusions. I did not believe that specific knowledge was reserved for a certain class of people. I think this inquisitiveness helped create a deep level of thought that is consistent with positive thinking; consistent with seeing the glass as half full, instead of half empty.

Another method of study I used is really a method of living. Challenging myself is necessary for growth, and doing that exposes me to knowledge. Since I developed the workshop version of *Success Is You*, I have continued to gather and analyze material. I wanted to assure myself that my conclusions continued to be subjected to new learning. I wanted to be sure that the experiences of the world's great thinkers and doers was considered. I needed motivational theory and application in its historical context, in its current usage, and in its future application.

My new reading included *Man's Search For Meaning* by Dr. Viktor Frankl. As I read the book my thought processes revolved around being thankful for what I have. I was reminded of complaining about having to start my power mower and mow my lawn. My complaint seemed reasonable until I looked across the street and noticed a one-legged man hopping behind a push mower.

While working on my Bachelor's Degree at Capital University, I had the opportunity to select a project that was applicable to my goals and purpose. I used that opportunity to enhance *Success Is You*. That enhancement occurred in several ways.

The first was to subject my basic concept to the scrutiny of the academic world and the business world. Step by step, my project went through the approval process. First was the preliminary approval. Then came the review by my Consultant, Mr. Ken Wilson and a mentor, Mr. Bertram Gardner. The project was drafted, reviewed, tweaked, twisted and practiced.

The final grade of ninety-six percent on the written project and one-hundred percent on the oral presentation left me elated and challenged. A ninety-eight percent average told me that the project was very good, but it reminded me that perfection is very elusive. In addition, I am probably my own worst critic, so I understand that *"I'm not there yet."* And when

I do *"get there,"* there will be yet another challenge.

The purpose of my project was to improve the belief level of the audience. The purpose was to cause the audience to want and to believe they could make positive changes in their lives.

The direct beneficiaries were the audience. The indirect beneficiaries are families, employers, co-workers and friends. The actions of human beings have a domino effect on others, the effects of which defy measurement and definition. We all are teachers, whether we choose to be or not. What we say and do, the examples we set, become words and examples that others live by.

I found that in **The Mismeasure of Man**, Stephen Jay Gould discredits the theories that would limit our potential based on Scientific Racism or other predetermined factors. In reporting on Gould's book, the **Saturday Review** states *"He stops at each point to illustrate both the logical inconsistencies of the theories and the prejudicially motivated, albeit unintentional, misuse of data in each case"* (Introduction).

It was Socrates who advised that *"Citizens should be educated and assigned by merit to three classes: rulers, auxiliaries, and craftsman."* He determined that a stable society *"demands that these ranks be honored and that citizens accept the status conferred upon them"* (Introduction Gould).

When Socrates asked Glaucon if there was a possibility that the citizens could be made to believe it, Glaucon's reply was *"Not in the present generation; there is no way of accomplishing this; but their sons may be made to believe in the tale, and their son's sons, and posterity after them"* (Introduction Gould).

And so the stage was set for man and woman to accept what I refer to as negative mental conditioning. Napoleon is reported to have stated that History is fables rewritten. As he shot the nose off the Sphinx, mental conditioning took on an expanded depth and meaning.

Negative mental conditioning, when allowed to flourish and become effective, neutralizes those abilities and that potential we have received from a higher power. We know not how different the world would be today, had all the possibilities to do good, been nurtured and come to pass.

With thanks to Gould and others who seek truth beyond the walls of separation, and with apologies to no one, I bring you conclusive evidence that Success Is YOU!

Spreading The Message
My Opening Remarks to The 16th Annual Conference of The Black Data Processing Associates

"You are the bandleader of your own parade. Until you sound your own trumpet, there will be no music to march to."

The following is from the 16th Annual Black Data Processing Associates (BDPA) Conference in Cleveland, Ohio. The date was Friday, August 19, 1994. The conference, which took place at Stouffer's Tower City Center, was a gathering of some of the country's top information system professionals.

I bring you the opening remarks from the 90 minute workshop that I did for BDPA on that day. I bring you these remarks because I need to assure you that *Success Is You* has relevance in the challenges facing individuals today. *Success Is You* is applied learning relevant to just about anyone who faces challenges. The lessons of life are the most appropriate remarks that I can share with my audience.

BDPA conferences are gatherings of those individuals who symbolize the message *Success Is You* brings. They are gatherings of winners who are making their footprints in the sands of success and making their mark in an industry where talent, competence, ability, flexibility, adaptability, resilience and persistence are prerequisites. It is to these individuals that I owe much of what I have learned and much of what I believe.

At this conference I was a lead-off presenter, scheduled to present at 8:30 a.m. the morning after BDPA's midnight cruise aboard the Nautica. So to those who were awake and ready for success, I bid,

Good Morning,

I am honored this morning to be among the first workshop presenters at the 16th Annual BDPA Conference. I am honored also that you chose *Success Is You* from among several workshops.

I think you recognize and I want to assure you, that *Success Is You* is applicable to you whether you are the *"New employee on the block,"* or a seasoned veteran. It is applicable whether you are an entrepreneur or employee, whether you are a line worker, staff member or management. Young or older, black, white, or red, rich or poor, it doesn't matter.

Success Is You deals with attitude, motivation and persistence. It deals with the basic ingredients we all need to formulate our recipe of success.

As I look at the theme *"Unleashing The Power of a Creative People,"* I am aware that a major challenge we face is believing that the theme applies to each of us.

We have the tendency through negative mental conditioning, or the lack of positive mental conditioning, to believe that the way things are, is the way they must remain.

We too easily accept the status quo. In addition to corporate America's glass ceiling, we build walls of resistance based on the limited vision others have of us, and we reinforce those walls with the limited vision we have of ourselves.

One major issue this workshop addresses is the need to alter your perception of yourself. You need to acknowledge your weaknesses only long enough to begin formulating a plan for corrective action. What is just as important is that you develop a deep appreciation for who you are right now.

We cannot all start life being better looking, or as the son or daughter of a multi-millionaire. We cannot all sing like Gladys Knight, dance like Michael Jackson, or look like Billy Dee Williams. We are who we are and where we are based 10% on circumstance and 90% on attitude.

It is only from this time and place that you can begin your journey of success. Don't apologize for who you are, but be proud. Don't ever say *"I'm only a Secretary,"* or *"I'm just a*

Data Control Clerk. "

Understand that the mistakes of a Data Control Clerk can *"bring down"* an MIS Director. Understand that an inefficient Secretary can cause major problems for a Vice President. Imagine that the President of a major corporation phones one of his or her subordinates, and that subordinate's Secretary says *"I'm sorry, but Mr. Jones said he's not in. "*

You see, the level of efficiency that exists within an organization is often determined by that individual having the lowest level of self-esteem and competence. It behooves each of us to radiate and surround ourselves with competence and confidence. I don't care whether you are a sparrow or a falcon, you cannot soar like an eagle if you're surrounded by turkeys.

One of the things we need to accomplish this morning is for you to share something about yourself with the entire group. This is not the time or the place to be shy about your accomplishments, or to be ashamed of your dreams. You can always say, *"the instructor made me do it. "*

Several years ago, a co-worker of mine responded to a newspaper article about me by saying *"I don't know about people who brag about themselves. "* I asked this co-worker how he contrasted true positive statements made in pursuit of a legitimate purpose, to barroom and poolroom conversations often made at the expense of feelings and reputations, and often while compromising the truth. The co-worker responded only with a look of disgust. A look that implied *"How dare I think and speak well of myself?"*

I could have asked the co-worker what he thought the purpose of a resume was, or what the purpose of a company's advertising brochure was. It was obvious though, that we were on different wave lengths. He was not tuned in to my frequency.

This co-worker paid none of my bills, fed me none of my meals, cheered none of my accomplishments. This co-worker was a member of what I refer to as *"The Small World"* a world that I will refer to later.

I need to know that you know, that until I started feeling good about and promoting myself, I wallowed in the mire of personal and professional stagnation. Until I began to beat my own drum, success was so silent a partner, that I could hear only the noise of my occasional failures. What I realize now is that failure was not my major problem. My major problem was not trying.

You are the bandleader of your own parade. Until you sound your own trumpet, there will be no music to march to. You have to decide whether your reward will be the acceptance by members of the small world, or the reward of self-fulfillment, self-actualization and success.

What is important to you? Is it the approval of those who don't know where they are, how they got there or why they're stuck? If you are uncomfortable with the emptiness of rationalization and the hollow sounds of *"coulda, shoulda, woulda,"* then you must dare to be different.

During the workshop I actually read my bio to break the ice and get the attendees to feel comfortable talking about themselves. I asked them to think of what they might like to see about themselves in print. I asked them to jot down everything, because later, if it didn't sound good, they could always scratch it out. I let them know about the coming publication of this book, and how they could have a place in it, if they would just open up and get beyond their fear of expressing their talents and abilities.

Please realize that you too must step outside your comfort zone and let people know who you are and what you are capable of doing. Hiding your talents and abilities does neither you nor the world any good. Bring out the real you and certainly you will begin to realize that Success is YOU!

- Section 2 -
Commitment and Character

What About You
Are You Willing To Believe?

If I Believe, If You Believe
We're Half Way There

The Path of Least Resistance
The Easy Way Can Hurt!

The Courage To Dream
Shrinking Mountains and Running Roadblocks

I Can, You Can
Attitude, Attitude, Attitude

Standards
Your Own Guiding Light

Honesty Is Still The Best Policy
The Reward of Being Able to Sleep At Night

Education and Training
A Lifetime Journey

What About You
Are You Willing To Believe?

"As a reader of this book you can become an achiever of tomorrow because of vision, because of attitude, because you have or are in the process of making a commitment."

What about you? Are you willing to believe in yourself to the extent that the losers in life will become uncomfortable with your accomplishments?   Understand that self perception and self development are so important, that little else matters. That's right, where you are now in your life has little to do with where you can go. Who you are has little to do with who you can become. The prerequisite for success comes from within.

Up to this point, I have given you my personal opinions regarding self perception and belief. My opinions however, were not produced in a vacuum, nor are they unique in the field of motivational theory and application.

Dr. Joyce Brothers, well known author, columnist and psychologist says

> *An individual's self-concept is the core of his personality. It affects every aspect of human behavior: the ability to learn, the capacity to grow and change, the choice of friends, mates and careers. It's no exaggeration to say that a strong positive self-image is the best possible preparation for success in life.* (Ziglar 49)

"God grant me the serenity to accept the things I cannot change, courage to change the things I can, and the wisdom to know the difference." That is an old but powerful and wise bit of advice.   I believe we place too many things in the first category.   A higher power equipped most human beings with five senses. There are many examples of successful people with less than five senses, Ray Charles, Stevie Wonder, Helen Keller. Having *all five senses* certainly implies that we have the capacity to be in control.

There is no practical reason to have a mind more complex

than the most powerful computer, and then let someone or something else dictate our future. I not only found this in books, but I believe it in my heart. Very often, you can't prove everything you feel, you just feel it. I can't prove to you that I have a large degree of control over my life, but if I stop trying, it will be easy to prove I am out of control.

So my challenge is to encourage you to improve your belief system, to believe in yourself and believe in a power greater than your own. Believing requires that often you just do what works most of the time, realizing that you won't always be right. It requires that you understand that life will not always be fair. It requires a belief that it is better to fail at trying to succeed, than to succeed at not trying. It requires that you understand, as Thomas Edison must have during thousands of failed experiments, that failure is just a temporary detour on the road to success.

It was Carter G. Woodson that said, *"If you can control a man's thinking, you do not have to worry about his actions"* (Brown 154). My purpose is not to control your thinking, but to encourage you to not let others do so. But if I am able to influence your thinking, I bring to you the assurance that the readers of this book can be the winners of tomorrow. You can be a winner without possessing superior intellect or unusual talent.

Eric W. Johnson, noted author and expert in achievement motivation said:

Achievers come in all races, nations, religions, cultures, climates, and economic groups. They include men and women, people with low IQ scores and high IQ scores, young people, middle-aged people and old people. (24)

Supporting Johnson's statement was Calvin Coolidge who stated:

Press on. Nothing can take the place of persistence. Talent will not; the world is full of unsuccessful people with talent. Genius will not; unrewarded genius is almost a proverb. Education alone will not; the world is full of educated derelicts.   Persistence and determination alone are omnipotent (Brown 39).

As a reader of this book you can become an achiever of tomorrow because of vision, because of attitude, because you have or are in the process of making a commitment.   None of us is born with the word "achiever" or "failure" tattooed on our chest. The hospital does not tag newborn babies with varying degrees of potential.   The experiences and reflections of life establish who we become, and therefore, we each are in control.

Again, I submit that you would have no need for your senses if someone else were in charge of your destiny. That is why it is reasonable for me to conclude that SUCCESS IS YOU!

If I Believe, If You Believe
We're Half Way There

"You have to believe that you are a recovering underachiever."

In the space available, I'm going to use myself as an example.   If I am to assume that the State of Ohio keeps records, somewhere in their archives is a sheet of paper called an aptitude test which bears my name. It is a test that tells me what I can do and what I can't do, and limits my belief of what is possible.

If I believe what I am told, I set artificial limits on my own potential. If I believe what I am told, I allow life to strike me out, without me doing as much as picking up the bat.

If I believe what I am told, I go to the grocery store, to the car dealership, to the housing market, crippled by the disease of *'don't have enough'* and the prognosis of *'can't get enough.'* I go with the mentality that my pockets and my mind are half empty rather than half full.

I then perpetuate stagnation and apathy among family, friends, associates and future generations of my descendants. We simply cannot afford to go through life not living up to our potential.

You have to believe that you are a recovering underachiever. You must understand that obstacles in the road of life are stumbling blocks to the pessimist, but stepping stones to the optimist.

You have to believe as Napoleon Hill expresses in his ten million seller, **_Think and Grow Rich_**, that:

> *You can be anything you want to be, if only you believe with sufficient conviction and act in accordance with your faith; for whatever the mind can conceive and believe, the mind can achieve.* (270)

You must realize that failure is a temporary detour on the road to success. You must realize that the rain that falls into your life teaches you to appreciate the sunshine, that without pain we would have no appreciation of relief, that without sadness we could not measure happiness.

Nothing I've done takes the brains of a rocket scientist. Everything I've achieved and more is within reach of most of the readers of this book.

The Path of Least Resistance
The Easy Way Can Hurt

"The skilled trades were still closed to minorities, based on rationalizations such as 'We only hire family members'"

One of the most potentially disastrous paths we can take on the road to success is the path of least resistance. There are many reasons we might take that path. We may do it out of laziness, or convenience, or because of false expectations or ignorance.

One false expectation of the 1950's was that young Black males, with few exceptions, were destined to become factory workers or semi-skilled workers at best. Very good and noble workers make up the population of factory and semi-skilled workers. The problem was that the widely held belief implied that there would be no other options. The basis for those expectations was a long history that could not be denied.

The effects of ***Brown vs. the Topeka Board of Education***, the Montgomery Bus Boycott and other historic events could not have been predicted. Even men and women of great vision and wisdom often underestimated the potential opportunity that was to come.

The practical result of what I have alluded to manifested itself as an artificially low *"upper limit."* It created a mindset that discarded the notion of being able to attain management and staff positions in business and industry. In line with these expectations, my educational route took me to Cleveland Trade School and training as an auto mechanic. Automotive maintenance was one of the few fields that Blacks could expect to get into. The skilled trades were still closed, based on rationalizations such as *"We only hire family members."*

At the time I entered Cleveland Trade, they did not award high school diplomas. Successful completion resulted in a certificate and the opportunity to serve a two-year apprenticeship. The school was renamed Max S. Hayes Vocational School while I was still attending. I finished school, but the apprenticeship never happened.

The mathematical result of subtracting the professional and skilled trades jobs that I could not have from a number already reduced by recession didn't leave a lot to choose from.

Taking the path of least resistance, based on the overwhelming evidence that I should do so, had a negative impact on my future. I was mentally trying to be that which I was not interested in, for the sake of convenience and conformity.

In this scenario, there is no one to blame, just a lesson to be learned. Your rewards in life are most often related to your willingness to consider the road which has the most stumbling blocks, for chances are there is less traffic on that road. Also, armed with the proper education and attitude, you may have the capacity to turn those stumbling blocks into stepping stones.

The Courage To Dream
Shrinking Mountains and Running Roadblocks

"Dreamers look beyond the limitations of what is and into the possibilities of what can be. Dreamers think and act beyond existing boundaries. "

That which we have not yet prepared for, we must begin to prepare for. That which we have not yet done, we must begin to do. That which we have not yet attained, we must visualize. Twice in 1992, I gave a presentation entitled *The Dream, Part II.* I have included a few comments from that presentation because of their relevance. *Dreamer* as defined by my computer software includes *"castle-builder, idealist and Utopian"* (PFS Software). Webster's New World Dictionary describes a dreamer as *"a person who has ideas or schemes considered impractical"* (Mish 382).

In all fairness, I must remind you that among the world's dreamers were The Wright Brothers. They had the nerve to defy the laws of gravity and the history of several thousand years. They had the nerve to visualize something that most sane men and women would have classified as insanity.

Because of their dream, because they rejected the paridigm that implies man must travel on the land or sea, the world of personal relationships, business, commerce and defense has never been the same.

Susan B. Anthony, the famous women's rights advocate, actually envisioned women voting. She challenged those who hid behind the shield of religion and those armed with the arsenal of law and terror and precedence. She had a vision, a dream, more powerful than the combined wit and wisdom of those who sought to deny her. And because of her, the Women's Equality Movement, even though it's not as well as it should be, is not as sick as it was.

Roger Bannister had the nerve to defy history and the predictions of experts in the field of physical limitation. He ran the first recorded four minute mile. Once he dreamed it and did it, he was followed by several thousand more in less than the next fifty years.

For thousands of years, that which was thought to be a physical limitation, proved only to be the crippling disease of Negative Mental Conditioning. Negative Mental Conditioning is a disease which manifests itself with the common symptoms of *"It can't be done."*

Dreamers come in all sizes and shapes and races and religions. Dreamers are in all fields of endeavor. What common attributes do dreamers have? Dreamers use their imagination to create a vision for the future. Dreamers look beyond the limitations of what is and into the possibilities of what can be. Dreamers think and act beyond existing boundaries.

Dreamers are willing to devote their time, their resources and their life to that which they envision. Dreamers reject the minimum daily requirement of just enough to get by. Instead they take large doses of education, training and positive mental conditioning. Their attitude and high level of persistence distinguishes them from others. Like Stephen Gould, they contradict the theory of predestination.

Henry David Thoreau, quoted in Les Brown's **Live Your Dreams**, says simply:

> *If you advance confidently in the direction of your dreams, and endeavor to live the life which you have imagined, you will meet with a success unexpected in common hours. You will put some things behind, you will pass an invisible boundary. New, universal, and more liberal laws will begin to establish themselves around and within you; or the old laws will be expanded, and interpreted in your favor in a more liberal sense, and you will live with the license of a higher order of being.* (221)

I Can, You Can
Attitude, Attitude, Attitude

" . . . .in your heart there is a passion and a fire that only you can light. "

I could not stand before 6000 people and deliver an alumni address that caused Keynote Speaker and former Congresswoman Mary Rose Oakar to question why she was needed, but I did. I could not go into a school and hold the attention and earn the respect of teens and preteens, parents and teachers, but I did.

I could not have received over twenty-five unsolicited letters of thanks for motivational speaking. These letters from students, parents, teachers, administrators and others are in contrast to my reality of low aptitude, no formal training and limited background. I should not be able to do what I am doing today, but I am.

Yesterday, I saw the glass as half empty, today I see it as half-full. Yesterday, I viewed the critics as casting the deciding vote, today I view them as having one more wrong opinion. Yesterday I lived a nightmare of mediocrity, today I'm working on my dreams.

In your mind, there are ideas that no one else has, in your background there are experiences that are unique to you, in your heart there is a passion and a fire that only you can light.

Just after belief and courage comes the simple but evasive task of making up your mind that you're going to do it, and keeping it made up, no matter what it takes. Once your mind is made up, you will need to be unusually single-minded and always relentless in pursuit of success.

The following, overheard at a national conference of information systems professionals, might well form the foundation of a positive attitude:

We could accomplish so much more, if all the grumblers would cheer up, if all the doubters would look up, if all the Christians would pray up, and all the cinchers would pay up, if all the gossipers would just shut up, if all the quarrelers would make up, if all the slowful people would catch up, if all the cold ones would warm up, if all the fallen ones would get up, if all the members would show up. (Unknown Author)

Attitude can be found in the story *The Little Engine That Could*, in the baby that is learning to walk, and in the ten year old that doesn't believe he is too small to play football with the teenagers. Attitude is a *major key to success*.

Standards
Your Own Guiding Light

Choose The Universe As YOUR Limit

Standards has a lot to do with attitude. In setting standards, I've developed the following philosophy:

The danger of choosing to be measured by the standards of others is that I may set artificially low limits on my own potential. If what is available to me is the combined wisdom of all who came before me, it is reasonable to believe that I can set new standards, standards which no one has yet dreamed of. Therefore I respectfully reject the limits you have set for me and in their place I choose the universe as my limit.

Honesty Is Still The Best Policy
The Reward of Being Able To Sleep At Night

"Sometimes life will knock you down and step on you so hard, that all you will have is faith. If you have always been a taker instead of a giver, what will be your level of faith?"

Much in line with the fallacy of instant gratification, are the stories of who *'got over'* the most by doing the least. Many of the exchanges are stories by people craving attention, and in some cases by people misinformed.

In other instances, people do not believe they can make it honestly. They lack a strong belief in themselves. They are the victims of negative mental conditioning and the hollow promises of instant gratification.

Everyone knows someone who got something for nothing, and temporarily appeared to escape the reality that you reap what you sow. We fail in the accurate analysis of these success stories because we don't have an adequate tracking system. Usually when people who tell us how easily they *'got over'* fall on their faces, their retractions are much quieter than their previous headlines.

What pops into my mind are two separate incidents that occurred where people proclaimed what a good tax angle they had. Just a very few years later, in very subdued voices made lower by bowed heads, they mumbled words to the effect *"Uncle Sam is really taking me to the cleaners. I've got to pay back ----. "*

Consider that these are the people that were honest enough to mention their mistakes. How many people are there whose claim to fame was made on a foundation of deceit, who would never come back and admit, *"I was wrong,"* or at least say, *"I got caught?"*

If we decide to live a life based on a shaky foundation, we should not be surprised when the walls come tumbling down. If we allow our road map to be prepared by those who do not acknowledge the quicksand of deceit or the hazards of illegal passing, then we are destined to pay the price of reckless living.

I am the type of person that would lose sleep wondering when *'they'* might come and get me. Looking over my back to avoid doing what I should do is too high a price to play the game of shortcut.

Be honest with yourself and others. A mind cluttered with the *"mental baggage"* of deceit cannot function with the clarity required to function at its best. A heart burdened by guilt will likely lack the strength needed to carry you through. Sometimes life will knock you down and step on you so hard, that all you will have is faith. If you have always been a taker instead of a giver, what will be your level of faith?

Education and Training
A Lifetime Journey

"Chart Your Own Course"

Famous Harvard psychologist Dr. William James, speaking on education said:

Let no youth have any anxiety about the upshot of his education, whatever the line of it may be. If he keeps faithfully busy each hour of the working day, he may safely leave the final result to itself. He can, with perfect certainty, count on waking up some fine morning to find himself one of the competent ones of his generation, in whatever pursuit he may have singled out. (Carnegie 82)

Education and training are major factors in success. I recently graduated from the Adult Degree Program at Ohio's Capital University and I now see education from a different viewpoint. It finally occurred to me that average was not sufficient if I could do better. I don't want an average house, I don't want an average car, I don't want to take an average vacation. I don't want average income when I retire, I am not communicating with average people. Average people usually don't read motivational materials.

"The average man," said noted psychologist, Professor Carl Seashore, *"does not use above ten percent of his actual inherited capacity for memory. He wastes the ninety percent by violating the natural laws of remembering"* (Carnegie 76).

The world is not looking for average people, except for those who will produce extraordinary results. In a message directed to Black Americans, but appropriate for all; Dr. Dennis Kimbro, co-author of *Think and Grow Rich, A Black Choice,* cautions; *"the entire world needs and is demanding a group of pioneers who have the capacity to conceive bold new plans, new ideas, and new visions"* (291).

The reason my high school average was in the range of 2.5 on a 4.0 scale and my average from community college was 3.41 and my average at Capital was 3.825, was not based on improved memory retention. The reason is not that I had less outside responsibilities or fewer concerns in later years. The difference is that education is no longer a destination; it's now a journey. It's because yesterday I believed statistics that defined my upper limits based upon race, gender and other broad categories and today I dare to dream.

Yesterday I allowed a distorted history to tell me what and who I was and how far I could go. Today I am making history because I realized that on this train ride called life, the conductor was not taking me where I wanted to go.

I realized that if I remained a passenger on someone else's train, I would always be behind, always catching the exhaust fumes, always going where someone else wanted me to go, and arriving at the destination when they thought it was time.

I urge you to build your own bridges, blast your own tunnels, establish your own path, take control of your own train, chart your own course, and do it at a speed that gets you to the next rest stop ahead of the crowd.

There is no distribution center in life which issues thoughts and actions. There is no K-Mart or Wal-Mart that sells them. Thoughts and actions are between you and your higher power and have nothing to do with the limited vision of others.

There are no easy payment terms. If you delay your first payment until spring, you delay the beginning of your growth until spring. There are no explicit warranties. You only have the implied warranty of self-assurance backed by the mental resources you develop.

- Section 3 -
Obstacles of The Mind

The Terrible T~~wos~~ *"Toos"*
Anyone Can Find An Excuse

Expectations and Reality
The Story of Robert Lee Booker, II

Failure, Risk and Reward
It's Only Safe In The Cemetery

But People Will Laugh At Me
And Other Excuses

Complacency
The Silent, Deadly Enemy of Success

The Terrible ~~Twos~~ *"Toos"*
Anyone Can Find An Excuse

"When mental stagnation takes place we avoid the destination of greatness by refusing to board the train of success."

Most parents think of the terrible *twos* as an age when infants, on their way to childhood, begin to seriously disrupt the peace and tranquility of the home. My definition of the terrible *toos* involves the crutch we use for failing to take charge of our lives. It is that period in our lives when we go from mental stimulation to mental stagnation.

When mental stagnation takes place we avoid the destination of greatness by refusing to board the train of success. We allow negative mental conditioning to dominate our thinking, to overrule our talents, our abilities and our dreams.

One of the challenges we face in becoming our best is to convince ourselves that success applies to us. We elude success by believing that we are either too young, too old, too black, or too white. Or we think its either too early or too late.

In response to being too young, I must remind you that before the age of 44, Joan of Arc reclaimed the territory of France and Martin Luther began the Protestant Reformation. When our nation was just an idea, an equally youthful Thomas Jefferson wrote the Declaration of Independence and Washington commanded the Continental Army. When we were a new nation, Madison fathered the Constitution, Hamilton served as Secretary of the Treasury, and Clay was Speaker of the House. In more recent history, John F. Kennedy became our nation's first Catholic President and Martin Luther King, Jr. stirred the nation and the world to a higher level of social conscience.

In response to being too old, let me remind you that after the age of seventy-five, Rosa Parks founded an organization to help young people become educated and self-reliant. Sharon Kelly, Mayor of Washington, DC, first entered politics in her mid forties, successfully challenging both the experts and the once invincible Marion Barry. Grandma Moses didn't begin to paint until the age of eighty. As I write these words, Mother Teresa continues to astound the experts by being an instrument of change around the world. As I write these words, Bob Hope and George Burns continue to entertain and enlighten audiences around the world.

In response to being too black, can education today be more difficult than being escorted into Little Rock's Central High School by 1,000 troops with fixed bayonets? How can today's struggles be more complicated than those of Benjamin O. Davis, whose classmates at West Point ignored him for four years, except in the line of official duty? If Jackie Robinson could see beyond the black cats and garbage tossed onto the baseball field, and go on to become a legend, then too black is a movable object.

When presented with the excuse of too white, I believe that someone forgot to tell Jerry West, Bill Lambier and Mark Price that they could not play basketball. They don't know that they can't do it, so they are doing it in spite of their *'limitation.'* Few people have the nerve to tell Fred Astaire and Arthur Murray they cannot dance. If you think that I have insufficient evidence for my conclusion, as my closing argument I draw your attention to the dancing in the movie *Saturday Night Fever.*

The terrible toos are stumbling blocks to the pessimist, but like other definable and movable objects, they are stepping stones to the optimist. You must ignore the excuses of those who build monuments of nothing. You have the capacity to look and step beyond the limits that others perceive for you. You can set standards no one else has yet dreamed of.

Expectations and Reality
The Story of Robert Lee Booker, II

"Hopefully, his example will establish an increased level of belief in you, in members of the 22.4% club and members of any group misjudged as inferior. "

As I was writing this book, <u>*Jet Magazine*</u> asked for readers to nominate candidates for the award of **Black America's**

Brightest Young Scholars. I had no problem thinking of Robert Lee Booker, II.

Robert had distinguished himself in a variety of ways. As a recent graduate of Twinsburg's Chamberlin High School, Robert graduated fourth in a class of over 170 students. His class ranking only began to define his exceptional level of talent and ability. He put his academic talents to good use by participating as a member of Academic Challenge.

Robert had been named Who's Who Among High School Students and earned the award of National Merit Student. He is a member of the National Honor Society. In addition to obtaining a full scholarship at the University of Notre Dame, Robert has been admitted as a Notre Dame Scholar.

Robert's academic achievements are matched by his ability and willingness to participate in extracirricular activities. His activities at his high school included being a member of the award winning Swing Choir, a drum major, member of the baseball team and the bowling league. The respect and admiration Robert enjoyed was evidenced by his selection as Vice President of the school band while at Chamberlin.

Robert did all this while holding a part-time job with a local business. I first met Robert while shopping at the store in which he worked. I came home babbling to my wife about this very personable young man that I had met. Dianne immediately knew whom I was speaking of, for she too had noticed him.

We were both amazed at his polite and helpful manner. He consistently displayed the persona of someone many years his senior.

Robert's strong family ties, his family's commitment and his perseverance are the things upon which his achievement is based. He has walked the path of success, in spite of the obstacles.

What I know about Robert established him as a positive role model. Even more meaningful is that Robert's accomplishments took place in an educational environment not totally supportive of minority students.

I should explain my perception that the local school system is *"not totally supportive of minority students."* The expectations of the system with regard to minority students is well defined in the following quote from *Your Twinsburg City Schools, Issue 4 - 1994*.

Twinsburg students had performed well in recent proficiency tests, but to explain why they didn't do even better, the paper stated:

> *We also have a very different demographic make up, with Twinsburg having a 22.4% minority population to Hudson's 2.2%. Quite frankly, many of our students are "over achieving" and should be commended.*

Quite frankly, to *be commended* is a questionable reward, when the other part of that reward is low expectations. Low expectations yield low results and I don't need to engage in a monumental research effort to support that position; it is a widely accepted fact. But Robert refused to be in the lower 22.4% of the class. He didn't care about demographics, he cared about Robert.

Hopefully, his example will establish an increased level of belief in you, in members of the *22.4% club* and members of any group misjudged as inferior. Hopefully, you too will begin to transcend the statistics, those little numbers that turn big possibilities into little probabilities.

Remember the statistics that said I could not be a speaker or a writer? The system failed to analyze me correctly, they failed to analyze Robert correctly, and if you put your mind and your heart to it, the system will be just as wrong about you.

My personal experience with the school system involves trying to be a good citizen and role model, particularly to the 22.4%, the *implied weak link*. I offered to speak at the local High School Commencement, citing my qualifications and my interest in giving something to the community in which I lived. My letters and phone calls were ignored until I went to a school board meeting. I was finally contacted, only after intervention by the School Superintendent.

The principal at that time, who is no longer with the system, coldly replied, without even a thank you, that the school didn't use outside speakers for commencement. A rather reasonable decision, but without even a thank you for my offer? It is not difficult to imagine why there is sometimes a reluctance to become involved.

Aren't some of the major problems confronting school systems, a lack of parental and community support? Isn't one of the cries sounded throughout the land, *"we need role models and examples for our students?"*

Wouldn't you suspect that the biggest need for role models would be for the 22.4%; the *implied weak link?* Wouldn't you think that a personal message from someone who defied the expectations and rose above negative mental conditioning might make the school system's job easier?

This nation has a pressing need for excellence in every area. On an individual level, lives are wasted and lost because of undeveloped potential. In becomes personal when I consider that our Goddaughter, Semora Burton and her sister Tabitha both attend the Twinsburg School System. Both are excellent students whose parents have instilled in them the need for education. Their parents, Ralph and Sherryl Burton, have set standards of excellence by example. It would be shameful for Semora and Tabitha's talent, ability and nurturing to fall victim to low expectations within the school system.

America cannot afford low expectations anymore than they can afford substandard performance. The number and quality of our future doctors, scientists, environmentalists, teachers, judges and everything else we are producing will be based upon our level of expectations. It is critical that we expect more students like Robert and Semora and Tabitha. I find it ironic that I only know three Black students in the Twinsburg School System and none of them fit the description of *low expectations.*

Robert Lee Booker did what I was not able to do, he showed the students and parents of Twinsburg what it is like to awaken a sleeping giant. He demonstrated in no uncertain terms that his upper limit was undefinable by statistics and graphs. He demonstrated that his challenge was not to meet the standard, but to set the standard.

As he goes about the job of being Robert, his finished product will be his personal accomplishments and rewards; the byproduct of which will be the critical element of hope for millions of unmotivated youth. Truly, the truth is the light, and Robert has lit the path for a generation of Americans that in many cases have been written off as lost. Thanks again Robert.

Failure, Risk and Reward
It's Only Safe In The Cemetery

"I would much rather be a failure at succeeding, than a success at not trying."

When you decide you're going to do something positive with your life, these little voices will ask, "What if this, what if that?" O.K., let's play WHAT IF?

What if Thomas Edison had said *"we've always used candles and lanterns before?"* What if Susan B. Anthony had been complacent in a male dominated society? What if Franklin D. Roosevelt had believed there was no defense against the Japanese Air Force? What if Rosa Parks had said *"That's o.k., I'll just stand?"*

What if I had listened to the aptitude tests that told me that I could not become a speaker or a writer? What if the other Henry Ford had given up on mass producing the automobile? How much would a $20,000 car cost if it wasn't mass produced?

The world would not be the same today if these people had chosen the comfort and safety of stagnation over the challenge of uncertainty. If we knew what could have been, but wasn't, because someone failed to challenge the unknown, we would be very upset, our lives would be very different. Yet often we make decisions to do nothing based on the fear or expectation of failure.

So what if you try and fail? The mathematical odds of failing everything you ever try to do for the rest of your life are staggering. And if you think that those odds are staggering, try to imagine succeeding without trying.

You didn't learn to talk without mispronouncing words, you didn't learn to walk without falling. Likewise, you won't succeed without trying.

The worst case scenario is that you never succeed at another thing in your life. But think of how much happier you will be for the rest of your life if you only believe that you will succeed. I would much rather be a failure at succeeding, than a success at not trying.

Failure is a learned concept that is more perception than fact. In the small mind, each of Thomas Edison's experiments that didn't work was a failure, but the light bulb was a success. We remember Edison's accomplishments, not his failures.

In the small mind, a baby falling while trying to walk is a failure, but the first step is the success. We remember the baby's first steps, not his or her failures.

So the failure you fear will be forgotten by others long after it continues to render you helpless. You must let go of fear and believe as Henry David Thoreau that, *"Nothing is so much to be feared as fear"* (Brown 131).

In his book entitled __Risking__, Dr. David Viscott said, *"If you cannot take risks on your own behalf, you are not your own person. You are your biggest problem"* (21). Dr. Viscott continues by saying

If you cannot risk, you cannot grow,
If you cannot grow, you cannot become your best,
If you cannot become your best, you cannot be happy,
If you cannot be happy, what else matters? (21)

We frequently think of risk as something related to mountain climbing, bungee jumping or going over Niagara Falls in a barrel. Other common forms of risk include trying out for a sports team or the cheerleading squad. You might fail. Learning how to ride a bicycle is a risk. You could slide a half a block on your face.

A boy asking out his first date, or any date, risks hearing the embarrassing word NO. A girl saying yes takes the risk of dating an oddball. Most people sometime in their lives have dated an oddball, but that doesn't stop them from dating. The point is that the fear of failure and the element of risk doesn't stop us from doing what we really want to do.

Somewhere between childhood and adulthood we learned how to be afraid. We learned how to play it safe, we learned how to stay on the shore, and then we wonder why our ship is not sailing. We must regain some of that youthful faith and confidence in our ability to succeed.

Most of the things we fear don't come true and most of the things we want elude us. There is a correlation between doing nothing and getting nothing. I suggest that if you keep on doing what you've been doing, you're going to keep on getting what you've been getting.

So don't let the villains of **What If, Fear** and **Risk** rob you of your just **Reward**. Living itself is a risk, so as long as you plan on staying, you might as well take some calculated risk. Remember that **It's Only Safe In The Cemetery**.

"But People Will Laugh At Me"
And Other Excuses

"Yes, it helps if the neighbor, the neighbor's dog, and everyone else you know approves, but that is frosting on the cake, it is not a basic ingredient."

Remember that the small world laughed as a group of colonists declared their independence from the most powerful nation in the world, but the big world smiled as the United States came of age. The small world laughed as Thomas Edison's experiments failed thousands of times, but the big world smiled as they saw the light.

The small world laughed as the young man from East 87th and Cedar avenue in Cleveland, Ohio challenged the so-called "Super Race," but the big world smiled as Jesse Owens received four gold medals at the 1936 Olympics. The small world laughed as a Catholic Senator challenged the status quo, but the big world smiled as John F. Kennedy became President of the United States.

Success requires that you become a member of the big world and that you ignore members of the small world. You aren't going to please all of the people all of the time, so you might as well begin by tuning out the small world.

What I have done in my pursuit of success has often been done without anyone's permission. What you must do in pursuit of your success needs the permission of just one person, and that is YOU. Yes, it helps if the neighbor, the neighbor's dog, and everyone else you know approves, but that is frosting on the cake, that is not a basic ingredient.

For most of my life, I haven't even been focused. That doesn't make me unique, it makes me normal. I have plenty of excuses to fail. The experts told me I probably would. I don't have a master's degree, my aptitude for speaking and writing is below 23%, as is my persuasive ability. I'm overweight and very thin on top.

Guess what, I'm going to be overweight until I'm thin and I'll be almost bald unless I buy a toupee. I'd rather be an overweight, bald-headed success than an overweight, bald-headed failure.

Don't rationalize and stagnate yourself into a life of failure. Excuses don't buy groceries and they don't fulfill dreams. I like Charles Swindoll's theory that life is 10% what happens to you, and 90% how you react to it.

In his book, *Man's Search for Meaning*, Dr. Viktor Frankl details his experiences of three years in Nazi's World War II death camps. These were camps in which he lost his father, mother, brother and wife.

Dr. Frankl went through that experience and went on to become a world famous psychiatrist and author of twenty books. The depths of his existence represent a low that most people will never experience, while the height of his accomplishments create a formidable and worthy challenge.

Like most people who overcome adversity, Frankl is not finished yet. When you have that kind of strength and vision and tenacity, even you don't know where your accomplishments will take you.

Frankl, in distinguishing several forms of neurosis, traces some of them to the failure of the sufferer to find meaning and a sense of responsibility in his existence. Frankl, in a common quote of Nietzsche reminds us that *"He who has a WHY to live can bear with almost any HOW"* (Preface XI). Nietzsche's quote was supported by American psychiatrists studying American soldiers both in Japan and Korea. Their findings were that those who knew there was a task waiting for them to fulfill were most apt to survive. Your *why* for living is that you haven't done all you came here to do, you have a meeting scheduled with SUCCESS.

Success is not a destination, but a journey; it is not a thing, but a way of thinking; it is not an accomplishment, but a way of acting. Success is a way of behaving, a way of living.

Complacency
The Silent, Deadly Enemy of Success

"Remember, someone is always trying to do it faster, better and cheaper. . .and that includes replacing you."

Many people have no desire to better themselves, will not set goals, they will not follow through. Many people won't open their minds and their hearts. Your taking the time to read this material tells me that you are not among these examples.

You have the ingredients for success. Don't sell yourself short. Don't overlook your assets, don't take them for granted. Without moving from your chair you're already ahead of 95% of the population.

Less than five out of one-hundred people will do any more about their dreams than talk about them. You've begun to do something about your dreams by reading this book, and I think you should acknowledge that.

Don't be afraid to congratulate yourself, because if you don't, no one else will. No one will benefit from your success as much as you, so no one else is going to do as much for you, as you. So like the song, *Give Your Baby A Standing Ovation,* you must always remember to give yourself a standing ovation.

If there was any single subject I could not leave out of this book, it would be the issue of complacency. One dictionary definition of complacency is *"self-satisfaction accompanied by unawareness of actual dangers or deficiencies."*

No matter how much education you have, no matter how smart you are, no matter what your level of expertise, you cannot afford to become complacent. Remember, someone is always trying to do it faster, better and cheaper. . .and that includes replacing you.

Even if all is well, change is guaranteed. Changes in politics, changes in how we do business, changes as dictated by supply and demand, and changes brought on by competition are just some of the changes you can expect. All these changes can have a negative impact on our goals and our career. Then there are changes *'just because'*. Yes I truly believe, that sometimes we just look too comfortable and complacent, and someone looks at us and decides, *"that person has it too easy, I'm going to make some changes."*

If you cannot sustain yourself without your present job and no one is knocking at your door with valid and respectable job offers, then you are not secure, you are complacent. If you are unsatisfied with any aspect of your career and you are not working on doing something positive about it, then you are complacent.

Often complacency has little noticeable effects on our progress. Each individual's circumstances are different, but the middle 1960's through the early 1970's was such a period in my life.

Prejudicial factors were less of a problem to many of us during that period. It was a time when during the heyday of the civil rights struggle, there was an emphasis on minority hiring. Many places of employment, including my own, had government contracts. There was investigation of civil rights violations and enforcement against violators, spearheaded by a federal government determined to enforce the law of the land.

Economic factors in our favor included the fact that America was a world economic leader, due in great part to industries such as automobile and steel.   These industries employed a significant percentage of minorities.

Competence factors in our favor included a strong discipline instilled by a struggling no nonsense generation of Black parents. Competence supported by parents who were determined that their children would succeed in a less than kind world. Competence supported by parents who knew that we had to be twice as good, just to break even.

Many factors were in my favor during the 1960's and early 1970's. The irony of complacency is that during good times it can strike even harder than during bad times. It is more difficult to recognize danger when all is well. The best defense against complacency is a good offense, for there is no vaccination or magic cure for it.   Whitney Young said *"It is better to be prepared for an opportunity and not have one, than to have an opportunity and not be prepared."* Once complacency finds you in a situation unprepared, your only recourse is to echo the infamous words *"coulda, shoulda, woulda."*

My own personal experience with complacency qualifies me to write about it with authority. In April of 1964 I became employed by a local manufacturer of screws, bolts and other hardware items.   Not a bad job during those times, and definitely as much as I might have expected given the limited amount of factory experience I had. After working there a year and a day, I secured a factory job with one of the choice employers in the Cleveland area.   It was a company called Euclid Division of General Motors.

Euclid Division's factory work force was represented by the United Auto Workers. In 1965 that went a long way in the grocery store checkout line. It meant good pay and benefits and it was to mean they were going to get even better.

Within one year of becoming employed at Euclid, I had gone through a seasonal layoff, been recalled, and received three promotions within the hourly ranks. Even my layoff was without pain. I received two immediate offers of employment with other General Motors plants, and in less than a week I received a third offer.

In 1966 I transferred to my first salaried position, that of Clerk-Typist. It required taking a reduction in pay, but I felt good about the move because I had gained substantial office experience while serving in the Army. That same year I began a two year Associate Degree program at Cuyahoga Community College.

In late 1967 I was promoted to Material and Parts Scheduler. By June of 1968 I was promoted to Computer Programmer Trainee. Success continued to be mine as I rode the waves created by a combination of good times for the auto companies and auto unions.

Standard operating procedure was to expect and receive pay and benefit increases comparable to those negotiated by the UAW. In addition, there were merit increases. Unions and management had discovered something called Cost of Living Allowance (COLA). Basically stated, the Cost of Living Agreement said that as the Consumer Price Index rose, pay automatically rose, and then they talked about the real raise.

I received an Associate in Arts Degree in 1973 and an Associate In Science Degree in 1974. I looked around and noticed that I had the same job as many graduates of four year colleges. It occurred to me that since I had been going to school for seven years, and was on top of the world, I didn't need any additional education.

I was overlooking implications of things such as the Arab Oil Embargo of 1973, and other events which were destined to change the standard of living in the United States. I had become infected with the disease that I now know as COMPLACENCY.

The symptoms of complacency are the same as the symptoms of success. A happy, full, satisfied feeling. The difference is that when you are complacent, you are not working on yourself.

By 1981 the benefits I enjoyed and had learned to take for granted had just about peaked. I'd had automatic wage or salary increases in most if not all the years since 1965. I had received merit increases in most of the years since 1968. I was receiving the automatic cost of living allowance. I had fourteen paid holidays, fully paid hospitalization, dental coverage, eye exam coverage, and nine SPD (special payment days).

Special payment days allowed you some combination of time off and/or additional pay based on a union management agreement. Again, that benefit, like most, was passed on to the salaried employees to maintain parity. It was as though someone left the door open and money and benefits just kept pouring in.

I call 1986 *"The year of Murphy's Law."* Murphy's Law states that what can happen will happen, and it did. By 1986 the factory I started in was gone, the cost of living allowance was gone, the special payment days were gone, and the visions of grandeur were gone. People were mumbling strange things like *"reduced medical coverage, employee cost sharing of medical benefits, etc."* I wished somebody had pinched me to wake me from the nightmare before they managed to take it all back.

Murphy's Law ruled the land in the 1980's. Numerous plant closings, the shifting of production facilities out of the U.S, reductions of staff sizes, givebacks, takeaways, outsourcing, foreign competition and the firing of Air Traffic Controllers.

All this along with the resulting union-busting mentality characterized ill winds in the making. I can remember some salaried employees who watched our manufacturing plant close and thought it was just happening to *"them."* Many could not believe that their own future was in jeopardy. They must have thought their white shirts were treated with layoff repellent.

While the economic reality of world markets reeked havoc upon America, the political climate reversed decades of workers' gains. Murphy was on the scene with a vengeance, I thought.

Over the years, although my place of employment did not change, my employer's parent company changed several times. We were sold and bought and acquired and merged. No big deal to the survivors. At least not the ones who were complacent. Anyway, as I write this book, the name on the pay stub I receive is Euclid, Hitachi, changed from VME Industries on January 1, 1994.

Murphy must have placed the Information Systems Department at VME on the top of his hit list for 1991. I will always refer to 1991 as the year of *"Murphy ain't finished yet."*

As if the economic downturn and foreign competition were not enough, it was announced that a portion of the company would be moving to Asheville, North Carolina, then the home of VME's U.S. manufacturing facility. In addition VME had an 11% personnel cutback in February, followed by a 10% cutback in June.

I decided that I'd heard enough bad news for one year, so I put in my yearly request to attend the Black Data Processing Associates (BDPA) conference. Since being named Cleveland Chapter BDPA member of the year in 1987-88, I had really been bringing VME's name to the forefront at every opportunity.

During speeches, when receiving awards, and at all kinds of affairs I shouted *"I work for VME."* Anyway, Murphy must have had a say in the approval process and he apparently didn't care anything about my unfolding future and community involvement.

VME decided they couldn't send me to the conference due to budget problems. *"WHAT?"* I shouted, *"but you can't allow me to go to New York City with no money, I'll starve."* Coming from someone too far over two hundred pounds to talk about it, my argument failed.

Even though I knew all conferences had not been eliminated for everyone, how much of a protest could I muster? The 21% of the former work force who now constituted the recently unemployed had other things on their minds, like finding a job and paying the bills.

I wasn't going to be denied though. I reasoned that I would use my merit increase to help pay for the New York conference. But management said, *"What merit increase? They have been frozen?"* You see now it was time to get mad, but I remembered that back in 1974 there was a young man who caught the disease of complacency, because all appeared to be well.

So who was I to get mad at? Our Japanese competition, the Arab Oil embargo of 1973, or the person who could have positioned himself just a little better in case the *"gravy train"* ran out of steam?

Oh, by the way, while I was figuring out whose fault this was, I found that if I survived the beating that Murphy was putting on me, the plans were in progress to outsource our computer mainframe processing to Volvo Data in Greensboro, North Carolina.

As I stated at the beginning of this chapter, this book could not have been written without a thorough review of complacency. What is important for you to realize is that this chapter is not textbook theory. It didn't come from a laboratory or from a chapter of a science fiction magazine, THIS HAPPENED!

Perhaps the most valuable asset you can receive is education from experience. What you learn from someone else's experience minimizes your chance of making the same mistakes. Most importantly, you avoid wasting the time.

Time is one thing that even money cannot buy. You have a certain amount of it in a day, and a certain amount of it in a lifetime. Please don't waste it being complacent, for I write with authority when I tell you that if you are fortunate to live long enough, you will eventually regret every complacent moment of your life.

- Section 4 -
A Matter of Perspective

Giving Success A Chance
Life Is Not A Three Minute Egg

Mediocrity
Versus Being Your Best

The Theory of 100 Percent Plus
Give At Least 110%

The Fortune Teller
From Stumbling Blocks To Stepping Stones

Professional Challenges
Rejection and Acceptance

Growing Through Networking
The Black Data Processing Associates As An Example

The Office Bigot
Represented by Ms. Ding Bat

Giving Success A Chance
Life Is Not A Three Minute Egg

"So to your education, attitude, persistence and vision, add the virtue of patience."

We live in an instant gratification society and we are conditioned to expect results almost immediately. While an *'Air Mail'* stamp used to designate urgency, we now are willing to pay almost $10 to send a single sheet of paper. Businessmen and businesswomen without faxes are looked upon as members of a weird cult.

The aroma of cooked cereal lingering for twenty-five minutes first gave way to the quick variety, and finally to instant. And even that isn't as fast as peeling rubber off the tires on your way to your nearest McDonalds. Heaven forbid if more than two people are at the drive-in window. We can't wait two minutes for breakfast, even if we have no dishes to clean afterwards.

Some marketing plans are sold on the basis of *"You can go from rags to riches in ninety days. Never mind learning business basics, just sign this application and buy these products and you will become Super Manager."*

The sacrifices necessary to be successful make it unlikely that everyone will get there. No, success is not likely to happen overnight, and you must begin preparing if you expect it to happen at all.

So to your education, attitude, persistence and vision, add the virtue of patience. It is a necessary ingredient in the recipe for success. Remember that the longest journey begins with a single step.

Mediocrity
Versus Being Your Best

"Life's ills and life's journeys require that you become the best that it is within you to be.

Regardless of what anyone else thinks of you, you don't have to settle for mediocrity. One of the most overlooked benefits of being your best is the reward of self-satisfaction.

Since I have decided to pursue my dreams at my pace and not wait for an evaluation designed to pay me enough to keep me, but not enough to satisfy me, I sleep very well at night. When I am challenged and criticized, I do as Frank Sinatra did. Sinatra decided that the best revenge against challenge and criticism was massive success and he began to act accordingly.

Action as opposed to words, positive as opposed to negative, best as opposed to better -- these are the goals you should seek.

Being your best is adequately summed up in the following example. If you had the need for a heart surgeon, you wouldn't want an average or a better one, you would want the best. If you could hire your own airline pilot, you probably wouldn't want the one who got a C+ in takeoff and landing, you would want the one that got an A. Life's ills and life's journeys require that you become the best that it is within you to be.

The Theory of 100 Percent Plus
Give At Least 110%

"The finish line of the loser must become the starting block of the winner. You must give your 100 percent plus, or learn to become a comfortable prisoner in the confines of complacency."

In a workshop I delivered entitled *An Urgent Agenda*, my challenge was to deliver a message designed to help people catch up. It focused on those who were behind either socially, educationally or financially.

The premise is simple. If you are behind in a track meet, you have to run faster to catch up. If you are behind in life, you have to get more education, develop a better attitude, become better trained, have more faith. The list goes on and on.

My audience in *An Urgent Agenda* were all Black and the workshop covered, among other things, the cumulative effects of

400 years of cradle to grave discrimination. More importantly, the workshop focused on constructive methods of overcoming the results of that discrimination.

I challenged the audience to visualize themselves in another time and place. I challenged them to think whether 100 percent effort would have been enough. The following two scenarios were used.

On the continent of Africa, when the forefathers of the slave were faced with the charge of a lion, or the pains of hunger, I asked whether anyone thought that the hunters ran or hunted at 75% of capacity. We all agreed that 100 percent plus was required.

In this country, when a slave had a chance to run, I asked did anyone think he or she ran at 75% of speed, and waited for a government assistance program to take over from there. Everyone agreed that the government program would have to run faster than 100 percent plus just to catch up with the former slave.

You don't have to be Black to understand the message I am conveying. The founders of this country did not escape the King of England by running only as fast and fighting only as fiercely as the English soldiers. It required 100 percent plus.

The immigrants who have come to this country in recent years, be they Mexican, or Asian, or Indian, have not made themselves comfortable working only as hard as some second, third and fourth generation Americans. They have done like the second, third and fourth generation Americans that are on the road to success. They have done 100 percent plus.

So the message should be clear. If you want to catch up or get ahead, you've got to do something that others will not do. As I stated in my workshop *Surviving Corporate America*, the minimum daily requirement may be fine for vitamin therapy, but it has no place on your march to success. On your journey you must be energized by a recommended daily allowance that others think is too much.

The finish line of the loser must become the starting block of the winner. You must give your 100 percent plus, or learn to become a comfortable prisoner in the confines of complacency.

The Fortune Teller
From Stumbling Blocks To Stepping Stones

"So you see, Fortune Teller, you told me the glass was half empty, when really it was half full. You wanted me to live in darkness, rather than learn to light a candle. You taught me about probabilities, but not about possibilities. "

What if I had believed my horoscope in 1941? Yes in 1941, the year I was born, the Fortune Teller came to the hospital room and said, *"Look son, let me tell you about your future. The Japanese are going to bomb Pearl Harbor, the Nazis are overrunning Europe and your father is a laborer who was born in the south. "*

The Fortune Teller said, *"Your father will pass before your 11th birthday; and you know single parent families don't work. Not only that, but your mother will contract multiple sclerosis about the same time. "*

The Fortune Teller continued: *"It's going to be thirteen years before the Supreme Court outlaws separate education and twenty-three years before this nation passes a civil rights act. And if you think that's going to solve your problems, some of your teachers aren't going to expect much from you. You're going to be told that you cannot pass algebra. "*

The Fortune Teller wouldn't stop: *"None of your family has been to college, and none works in an office. You could learn a trade, but when you go to Max Hayes Vocational School, you are going to be threatened and harassed. When you graduate in 1960, the unions aren't going to accept you. And in 1960, Max Hayes won't be awarding diplomas yet, so all you will have is a certificate of rejection. "*

The Fortune Teller finally said, *"Well I think you're sufficiently depressed, so I'm going to go find my next victim and tell them why their life will be useless. I'll be back to work on you later. "*

"And while I'm gone," said the Fortune Teller, *"don't even think about getting a GED diploma or getting a good*

paying job in Corporate America. Don't try to start your own business. Your sales aptitude is in the nineteenth percentile. It won't work!"

"Don't think you can learn anything about investments; and you'll never know enough to earn an Investment Education Award" the Fortune Teller shouted. *"Remember, you can't even pass algebra, how do you expect to learn anything about balance sheets? Your world of higher finance will be counting your earnings from a job at McDonalds"* the Fortune Teller said.

The Fortune Teller said, *"As late as 1985, while house hunting, you're going to be stopped on the tree lawn by four people who tell you the house has been sold. You're going to find out a week later that there hasn't even been an offer."*

People on a mission of success talk back to their Fortune Teller. Yes, Fortune Teller, I said, there was a war, and as tragic as it was, it created jobs and economic revitalization. Out of necessity, it brought together people who had for years been divided.

It made of the United States the economic, industrial and military leader that was within its capacity. Hopefully it brought to our minds and placed into our hearts the knowledge and the will to do it more compassionately the next time.

And my Blackness is a source of survival, not an excuse for failure. Yes, my father was a laborer, but for ten years he taught me the strength of silence and kindness and persistence.

While traveling to my father's boyhood home in Georgia, the restaurants which would not accommodate me taught me the goodness and the economy of a *"shoebox lunch."*[1] The environment of exclusion taught me to be grateful for the small things in life and ecstatic for the bigger things. It taught me that the good life was a goal to be achieved, not a thing to be handed down.

Yes, my father passed before my 11th birthday, but I had him for ten years more than many and wouldn't have traded him for any. My mother's illness taught me caring and compassion in a way no college professor could.

The few teachers that expected little were overruled by a mother that expected much. Certainly, I was not wanted at Max Hayes, or at the union office, or in the plush offices of The Fortune 500, or in most neighborhoods.

Sometime when you're not wanted anyplace and you've got to go some place, you do what is necessary. You develop a strength and a vision like the Apostle Paul, to call forth those things that be not, as though they were. You learn to walk by faith, putting that which you cannot control in the hands of a higher power.

So, Fortune Teller, I went to college anyway and prepared for opportunities that were not available. I did what those before me had not done, because I was becoming who I am today.

I understand that the illness of discrimination will not be cured with a vaccination of legislation. I've decided to use the antidote of a strong heart and a made up mind and focus on who I can become instead of what I am being denied. I started my own business as a diversion to the glass ceiling you warned me about. In the midst of doing what the aptitude tests told me I could not do, I started to become better and better and better.

So unlike the man who was given a castle with no foundation, I built my home from the ground up. A strong family background and faith are the foundation of my house. That foundation will withstand the pressure of turmoil and change. The walls of my house are reinforced with education and training to hold off the bitterness of temporary defeat.

My developed and sharpened mind is the roof of my house, a roof that protects me from the fallout of the jealously and the misdeeds of others.

My house is insulated with warmth and patience. When the chips are down and as my mother used to say *"it's too warm in the frying pan and too hot in the fire,"*[2] I've developed a head cool enough to air condition my house.

If I truly cannot do something, I'll find out. So I no longer need the services of an aptitude test maker. They're fired! I don't need him or her if I want a reason to succeed, I only need them if I'm looking for a reason to fail.

And you're right, Fortune Teller, in 1985 I was met by a lady and three men at the curb, telling me that property was unavailable, reminding me of a time I would just as soon forget. So I didn't get a home in South Euclid, I got one in Twinsburg. My second presentation of the workshop, *Success Is You*, was part of the Twinsburg Adult Education Program. If I hadn't lived in Twinsburg, I probably would not have had that opportunity. So my point is, I have to believe that I ended up where I was supposed to be.

Sometimes we have to take the long route to get to where we ought to be, sometimes we must have faith. If the road to a happy and fulfilling life were wide and straight and well lit with a comfortable downhill grade, everyone would get there. The truth is, the road less traveled has detours and obstacles and dangers, but also has the most opportunities.

So you see, Fortune Teller, you told me the glass was half empty, when really it was half full. You wanted me to live in darkness, rather than learn to light a candle. You taught me about probabilities, but not about possibilities.

I now have fifty-three years experience turning stumbling blocks into stepping stones. During those years, I have become tired of being a victim of your predictions. I have developed a plan of action, and like psychologist and philosopher Dr. William James, I believe that if you *"Sow an action, you reap a habit; if you sow a habit, you reap a character; if you sow a character, you reap a destiny* (282)."

So, Fortune Teller, in this era of outsourcing and downsizing and cost cutting, I can no longer afford your philosophy of life by accident, I am seeking a life on purpose. The job classification of Fortune Teller has been eliminated. You're fired!

Everyone has a Fortune Teller, everyone has excuses as to why they can be a failure, but we all have reasons why we can become successes. Fire your Fortune Teller; you don't need anyone or anything to hold you back.

Professional Challenges
Rejection and Acceptance

"The thing you must remember and you must demonstrate in both words and deeds, is that YOU like YOU."

When I entered the field of data processing, since known as management information systems (MIS), information systems (IS), etc., the time was June 1968. My feelings at that time can best be described as anxious. Only six months before, I had been promoted from sr. clerk to material and parts scheduler.

I wasn't particularly fond of the material and parts scheduling job. Looking back, I understand that I didn't have the faith that I could do it. Remember Negative Mental Conditioning? Also, I wasn't prepared for the temporary defeats associated with missing critical deadlines. I lacked the support system that would have told me that failure is a prerequisite to success.

General Motors, our parent company at the time, had agreed to sell our unit as part of an antitrust settlement. I decided to apply for a job within the new parent company. I was hired as a computer programmer trainee. So I had a title I could barely spell and a job I knew nothing about. I only knew that I wouldn't be scheduling parts that almost never arrived on time.

Computers were still relatively new, and the chances of me finding a retired or working computer programmer in my old neighborhood were not <u>next</u> to none; they <u>were</u> none. I don't remember if the term mentor had been coined in 1968, but if it had, it didn't matter, because I didn't have one.

So what do you do when you almost accidentally become part of a new high tech field, in a world of old ideas? What do you do when you have a responsible position that many people don't think you can be trained to hold? What do you do when many people think you are a quota, and you've been educated and conditioned to believe that your upper limit was simply to get a job?

If you're like I was, you sweat and pray a lot. Since I've now been through what I've been through, I still sweat and pray, but now I do it with a faith and a vision that I am able, willing and ready. It wasn't like that in June of 1968.

It was my good fortune that a White co-worker by the name of Howard Ivary was willing to guide me over many of the rough spots, because I was totally confused. Other members of my department including John Trevis, Ken Siembida and Tom Kennedy also gave me a great deal of help.

Within my department, there seemed to be a reassuring level of acceptance, so I survived. Outside the department however, circumstances arose that reminded me that all was not yet well in America.

On occasion, the poison of discrimination found its way into my system. Sometimes it was in such a small dose that I had to think about it.

Sometimes it came in stronger doses, lacking so in thought and consideration that I wondered who were the real educated and enlightened. Like the time a co-worker wanted to make a point of how low a particular young lady's moral standards were. *"She even dated somebody Black"* he moaned. His voice expressed a pain that would have made you think he was on his deathbed, besieged by a lethal mix of all the world's plagues.

At other times discrimination dealt such a crippling and painful blow that its carriers revealed the full side effects of ignorance and stupidity. Sometimes it was so blatant that I had to wonder if the lynch mob was on its way from the parking lot.

Just so the reader doesn't think I'm paranoid, I need to share one experience that involved someone that I had liked and respected. I was in a meeting where this individual was present. As the information systems representative, my task and challenge was to accumulate facts, so that I might offer an effective and cost-effective solution to the problem at hand.

In those days, being new on the job, I did a lot of listening, a habit I have tried to keep. I was doing my job so quietly that this person, possibly forgetting I was in the room, blurted out a possible solution to a production problem.   *"Give the job to the niggers, because it will cost us less,"* said Mr. Newly Found Out Bigot.

The remark would have been easier to accept coming from an acknowledged bigot. Coming from one who spoke to me each day and smiled, the remark assured me that all was not well in America. It made me realize also that I didn't even know who had the disease.

War and conflict are bad enough when you know the enemy, but its pure torture when you don't. Being the optimist and looking back, I understand that this person helped prevent me from becoming confused about who I was.

The message to the reader doesn't have to be steeped in the stench of racism or sexism or any other sinful practice. The point is that it doesn't matter who you are, or what position you hold. Whether you are black or white or yellow, you need to understand that there are some people out there that don't like you, and won't like you no matter what you do.

Some people have a dislike for short people, some for tall people, some for fat people and others for skinny people. Some don't like baldness, and others can't stand long hair. The list goes on and on, but so does life.

What is the best defense against discriminatory behavior? The best defense is an educated, well-trained, competent, motivated, persistent, determined Y-O-U. Everyone won't like you, no matter who you are or what you do. The thing you must remember and you must demonstrate in both words and deeds, is that YOU like YOU.

Growing Through Networking
The Black Data Processing Associates as An Example

"Sometimes, when you haven't been invited to 'play' with the 'Good Old Boys' you need to locate, build, participate in, your own network"

During my years in information systems, my exposure to other Blacks was limited to one other co-worker at a time, and then only on those rare occasions when we were operating near 100% of staff.

The exposure to females was numerically better, but the *'Good Old Boy'* network prevailed. One White female co-worker was told by our director that he was putting her in charge temporarily *"until he could find someone qualified."* Fine, let's blame the female for the results, even though the director claimed she didn't have the skills to be responsible.

Just about the time I began to feel like the Lone Ranger, and like information systems was simply a reflection of computerized tokenism, I met someone who was to have a profound impact on my life.

Ken Wilson grew up in the same neighborhood that I lived in during my late teens. His sister Linda and my sister are still friends, separated only by miles. As life would dictate, I didn't meet Ken until the early 1980's, while attending a class. As life would dictate, I met Ken when I needed to. Ken was and still is a member of the Cleveland Chapter of The Black Data Processing Associates (BDPA).

Ken has held several offices in the local chapter, including several years as President. He has also held several national offices while simultaneously running a successful business. He has always been a quiet, concerned and effective role model.

BDPA has been instrumental in my increased confidence and belief in myself. In addition, I have met many people who count themselves among the winners in life. I first heard Les Brown at a BDPA national conference. I have conducted several workshops for the organization and held several positions on the local executive board. I have done things within BDPA that by design or circumstance have been denied me in corporate America.

I didn't do what I did for the money, because BDPA is a volunteer organization. What I want to impart is that my growth in experience, confidence, and community involvement has paid immeasurable rewards. Of all the money I made in Corporate America, it would not purchase the confidence necessary to sustain me.

We grow from people and projects, and your professional development sometimes requires that you step outside your comfort zone and into uncharted territory. Sometimes, when you haven't been invited to play with the *'Good Old Boys,'* you need to locate, build, participate in, your own network. You need a BDPA or some group to develop and enhance your professional growth.

My first exposure to BDPA was to have the opportunity to address them regarding the benefits of the National Association of Investors Corporation (NAIC). It seemed only fitting that Black professionals were those people who had both the need and the open-mindedness to hear what I had to offer. Even though my nervousness probably showed through, I was thanked and applauded, and I received a welcome much warmer than I had expected.

I was extended an invitation to join BDPA, but I felt that my unfinished business with NAIC, my full time job, and part-time business interests were enough to keep me more than busy. I declined membership at that time because BDPA appeared to be an organization of doers, and I didn't want to be dead weight on a membership list. Several years later, circumstances which I cannot even recall found me back at a BDPA meeting, membership application in hand.

Upon becoming a BDPA member, I almost immediately found out why they get things done. Almost before the ink was dry on my application, I somehow found myself as membership chairperson of the Cleveland chapter. The experiences I encountered within BDPA have been numerous and diverse, and very valuable.

As membership chairperson, I developed a membership manual which has been used as a model for several chapters nationally. In an attempt to develop something to help me do a more effective job, I received national recognition. It was just that natural and that simple.

In addition to membership chairperson, I had the opportunity to serve as corporate relations chairperson, an *ad hoc* committee formed at my suggestion. I also served as communications chairperson. Part of my duties in that capacity was to serve as editor of **_Data News_**, which at that time was the official publication of the Cleveland Chapter.

I was also honored to have been named Cleveland Chapter Member of The Year in 1987. The honor meant so much because I recognized the talent, the dedication and the sincerity of the other candidates for that honor.

There is not enough room for all the details, but I can state without reservation that my BDPA involvement has been instrumental in my growth as an individual. The goals of the organization include the education, training and motivation of everyone in general, and minorities in particular. The members are people working in a variety of positions within the information systems area, and other fields such as accounting, sales and marketing.

The networking opportunities to enhance knowledge and skill are plentiful, as is the opportunity to contribute to the betterment of humankind on levels you probably never thought possible. Many opportunities for employment are a natural byproduct of maximizing your potential, becoming aware of the talents of others, and of others becoming aware of your talents.

BDPA's programs span a variety of topics of interest not only to information system professionals, but to anyone seeking to make a better life for themselves. Programs cover areas such as motivation, economics and supervision.

One of BDPA's most important and visible functions within the community is that of providing the opportunity for young people to become exposed to information systems through workshops, computer competition, and other activities. Also, contrary to my original concerns, BDPA involvement will not label you a revolutionary.

On the contrary, knowledgeable people in the business community will recognize your association as positive. You will be assumed to be a highly motivated, caring, concerned and involved citizen of the community. You will represent a mirror image of the type of individual that knowledgeable employers are looking for today.

BDPA has grown dramatically since its founding in 1976. There are currently over 44 chapters nationwide. As part of the process of coming of age, the organization and its members enjoy widespread acceptance. There is now major corporate support from those who understand that BDPA has the ideas and programs necessary for survival into the next century.

The Office Bigot
Represented by Ms. Ding Bat

"What the bigot has to threaten us with cannot equal what we have already endured."

The office bigot may hatch in the form of someone who always has a Black joke, or someone who simply thinks that you are the spokesperson for any Black person who is lazy, shiftless, criminally inclined or any other negative things.

The office bigot likes to put you on the defensive; they want to make you accountable for that for which you have no accountability. They almost always ignore anything positive about any Black person. At best they are an irritating distraction.

The office bigot doesn't have to work in an office. Their ignorance transcends all of business and industry. They can spew their venom equally well whether on a construction site or in a plush office.

Ninety-nine percent of the cases involving the office bigot can be resolved by outsmarting them. Outsmarting the office bigot is not normally the greatest challenge in the world, because the time they spend putting you down cannot be used to lift themselves up.

Don't resort to their level of gutter mentality, because you will then become a part of the problem. Remember that they have to keep reminding you of your supposed inferiority for one reason. That reason is because they aren't really sure of it themselves.

Don't employ a physical response to the office bigot unless you are in physical danger. You will more than likely be assumed to be the provoker. Remember who the likely judges are.

Use a tape recorder where possible and appropriate. Don't expect an unbiased group of witnesses to convene in your behalf. People not subjected to constant racial or sexual discrimination and abuse cannot relate to it. Their response is usually *"I didn't hear it," "Maybe he didn't mean it that way," "You are so sensitive."* These people have no perception of what it's like going through this almost daily, from the cradle to the grave. Sometimes I even find it hard to believe.

Project the same pride in your race that has been projected since the dawn of history in this country. Make your initial goal to be as good as the best, pausing only briefly before setting the goal of being better than the best. Don't let others confuse you into being as bad as the worst.

Understand that discrimination is as old as mankind, and your talents and abilities will likely be wasted attempting to reason with the perpetrator of racial hatred and insensitivity.

Understand that we were brought to this country in chains and then accused of being the savages. Understand that we were lynched and beaten and abused, and then charged with the crime of trying to escape. Understand that we were denied the right to vote, and then accused of not being patriotic.

Understand that we have been denied education, and then been blamed for being uneducated. Understand that we have been denied the right to adequate rest facilities, and then been blamed for being untidy. Understand that we've been denied employment and union membership, and then been blamed for not working.

Understand that if we are still here after all this has happened, that we have a reason for being here. Understand that some people just can't or don't want to understand.

It is not only our right, but it is our duty, to let the bigot with diarrhea of the mouth, coldness of the heart and constipation of the brain, wallow in their own discontent -- by themselves.

While the bigot spends time implying his or her membership in a "super race" and implying that you are a non-entity, the challenge to you is to prepare yourself for the next opportunity.

If you don't remember anything else about the office bigot and all the big bigots and little bigots and the whole bigot family, remember that **WHAT THE BIGOT HAS TO THREATEN US WITH, CANNOT EQUAL WHAT WE HAVE ALREADY ENDURED.**

We simply can't ignore the office bigot. Any group who has made so many so miserable for so long, needs their day on the chopping block. I won't go so far as to say there is one in every office, but I can categorically assure you that there are more than enough to go around.

The office bigot comes in all sizes, shapes and temperaments. They even come in all colors. My particular experiences included those who have a large quantity of Polish or Black jokes. It includes those who thought that I should be able to explain the negative traits of all Black people. It includes those who can't believe that I could have any positive traits.

The office bigot is often multi-talented, able to ignore logic with a single sentence. Office bigots have aspirations too. Some office bigots want all foreigners to go back to Africa or Asia or wherever, while they want to stay and continue to *'protect'* the Indians.

A good example of how we can use the words and actions of the office bigot to work in our own behalf is reflected in the following true story of Ms. Ding Bat (alias), whom I'll refer to as Ding for short. Ding was a co-worker of mine who seldom if ever let an opportunity go by to speak negatively of some Black person who shot, stabbed, mugged or in some other way abused somebody.

Ding felt that I had a unique ability and a moral responsibility to explain all the negative or questionable actions of Blacks. I was never asked to explain the words or deeds of Dr. Ronald McNair, Susan L. Taylor, John Johnson, Bill Cosby or others who made a positive and recognizable impact.

A typical one of Ding's comments was made when a popular Black Cleveland Browns football player whom I'll call

Mr. X got into trouble with the law for allegedly selling drugs. Without any rhyme or reason, Ding begins the conversation with *"Henry, since you're black, maybe you can tell me why Mr. X sold drugs?"*

As long as Mr. X was on the football field doing his job, thrilling thousands and making millions, I wasn't asked about him. All of a sudden when he was in jail and in trouble, I was elevated to the status of his brain, conscience and mouthpiece. My total relationship with Mr. X consisted of the fact that I was of the same race, something that was decided by a power much greater than myself or Ding.

What is important for each of us to realize is that Ding's non threatening but socially irresponsible behavior over the years made me a wiser and stronger person. Not only did I never forget that one of my missions in life was to improve conditions for myself and others, but I was constantly reminded of one of the obstacles.

I never let my guard down and there was always mental preparation prior to confronting Ding for another day. Any time the disease of complacency was about to set in, there was Ding bringing up something totally irrelevant to anything positive.

I consider my experience with Ding something like going to get a vaccination. Like any painful experience, you don't look forward to it, but it toughens you and you become a better person because of it. Beyond that, my totally lopsided conversations with Ding have given me information to share with you.

Since I have begun to do motivational speaking and write books and articles, I have been able to use Ding as an example often. Therefore in the greater scheme of things, Ding actually helps me to live my dreams.

Life Is A Game
Play It Like A Professional

"Your best chance is to be well prepared and patient. Don't take wild swings and reckless chances, but remember that eventually you must take a swing."

Some days it seems like it doesn't pay to get out of bed. Others days you wonder why things are going so well. Life is just like that. As one of my former programming managers used to say, *"Some days you get the bear, and other days the bear gets you."*

I realize that I cannot separate where I am from the experiences of life. Sometimes we want to sit down and figure out how to not make any more mistakes. When I look at where I am personally and professionally in my life, I realize that even the most sophisticated computer could not have predicted where I would be at this time.

Being a writer and speaker may not have happened if I had not met Les Brown. That may not have happened had I not gone to the BDPA National Conference in Chicago in 1988. I may not have known about BDPA had I not met Ken Wilson. There is a direct path of circumstance leading back over the road I have traveled, without which I might not be at this destination.

In addition, all the detours and interchanges along the highway of life have in some way altered my destination and my arrival time. I'm not going to try to figure it out, it's too complicated. What I must believe until someone can prove otherwise, is that persistence in pursuit of worthy goals increases the probability that you will get where you want to go.

Life does not come with a money back guarantee. You cannot buy an extended warranty beyond healthy living habits and a reasonable degree of rational behavior. You cannot get a refund or a replacement. You cannot put life into "will call," and then resume living when conditions get better.

You are stuck with what you have, and you will just have to do it, do it, do it! Try to do what you know is right all of the time, and when you slip up, don't throw in the towel. Admit your mistake or your shortcoming and dig in for another try.

Life will not feel sorry for you if you give up. Life will not wait for a teammate to consult with you on the mound. Life offers no seventh inning stretch. No one can pinch hit for you, and there is no bullpen to rely on. You are the entire team.

As a pitcher, you must throw life your best pitch. As a catcher, you must handle the curves life dishes out. You must become quick enough for the fastball and tough enough for the hardball. When you play the bases, you will sometimes make an error, but with practice comes improvement, and you can eventually expect more double plays and even an occasional triple play.

In the outfield you will often be lonely, but your position will still be important. When you least expect it, you will be called upon to be the backup to what someone else has missed. Opportunity will sometimes come your way low and fast, and other times it will come high and slow. It will be up to you to remain alert and be ready and willing to adjust your speed.

Sometimes the catch will be easy and other times you will be required to stretch beyond the limits that you considered possible. You may be blinded by a relentless sun, or fooled by the winds of change. But be assured that most of the time, if you give it your best, it will soon be your turn at bat.

When it is your turn at bat, when you step up to the plate, all eyes will be upon you. Some will be hoping you hit a home run, others will be praying that you strike out, and many won't care. Remember that it is your ball game. You will receive very few perfect pitches. Much of the time you will have to make the best of what life throws to you.

Your best chance is to be well prepared and patient. Don't take wild swings and reckless chances, but remember that eventually you must take a swing. Remember your training and keep your eye on the prize. Despite all your preparation, sometimes you will strike out. Don't let that deter you, because preparation and persistence will insure that your batting average will see you through.

- Section 5 -
Winners, Winners, Winners

Winners By Choice
Several Successful Businesses

Examples of Excellence
Looking Into The Mirror and At The 1994 BDPA
Conference Attendees

Others On The Move
The New Generation of Entrepreneurs
and Their Success Stories

Profiles of Inspiration

The Extended Family
Success Multiplied

In The Presence of Greatness
And You Probably Don't Even Know It

Winners By Choice
Several Successful Businesses

"Common individuals faced with the challenges of life and responding to those challenges by moving steadily and resolutely toward success, will achieve that success with astounding regularity and with commendable results"

There are many success stories about *'average'* Americans, often producing extraordinary results. Most have never been and probably never will be told. This section shows the relationship between the principles of success and reality. The most difficult job was deciding what stories not to use.

The Artisan Emporium
Dorothy Banks, Paula Banks, Mittie Gamble

Thanks to the knowledge, foresight, and tenacity of three enterprising ladies, the city of Cleveland in general, its African American community in particular, and the entire nation are culturally richer.

The Artisan Emporium Gallery is beneficial not only to those African American artists whose work is represented, and to those collectors actively seeking African American art, but, in addition, the presence of this unique business gives hope to the countless thousands of Cleveland area residents, who otherwise might never have been exposed to the beauty and quality of Black art.

The stated purpose of the Artisan Emporium, as described by the founders, is as follows:

"The Artisan Emporium Gallery was created out of the need to showcase works of African American artists. African American art has generally been neglected in art circles. The Artisan Emporium Gallery is the first of its kind in Cleveland. We have opened the doors of opportunity to artists who are not well known both locally and nationally. Our venue is to educate the Black

community regarding works of African American artists. Also, to impact on positive images for young African Americans.   We want to establish an inviting, non-institutional setting to display artwork.   This will enable the public to enjoy the art, thereby, moving them towards wanting the artwork in their environments.   The Artisan Emporium Gallery is more than just a gallery, it is a center for creative expression encompassing all of the arts such as: visual arts, writers and Afro-centric artifacts.   For more information about art, artists, and exhibits contact the Emporium at (216) 383-0809 or stop by and see us at 18013 Euclid Avenue, Cleveland, Ohio 44112. "

In addition to the explicitly stated goals and objectives above, a deeply rooted implicit value of the Artisan Emporium to the community is that it serves as a pleasant reminder of the many and varied talents within the African American community, and is therefore a significant asset, even to those who have yet to develop an appreciation of art. I am happy to have become acquainted with the Artisan Emporium, and as a result, I have become more aware and appreciative of the multi-talented members of the Artisans Guild.

Foster Enterprises
Dr. Rodney N. Foster

Dr. Rodney Foster is a practicing dentist with offices in Shaker Heights, Ohio. A graduate of Ohio State University, and the School of Dentistry at Ohio State University, Dr. Foster is also the President of Foster Enterprises, a growing organization in the rapidly expanding field of network marketing. In addition, Dr. Foster served two terms as the President of the Forest City Dental Society. He is the proud father of Rodney Jr., Angela, and Lauren Ashley.

I am fortunate to have known Dr. Foster since the age of five. We grew up together, lived four houses apart, attended

Cleveland's Doan Elementary and Empire Junior High Schools at the same time, had the same teachers, and received similar grades.

Dr. Foster's path led him to Cleveland's Glenville High School, and then on to undergraduate studies and eventually to the School of Dentistry of Ohio State University. I often wondered what gave him the vision at such a young age, while some of us, his former playmates and classmates, took many more years to develop that vision. And many of us still don't have it.

When I asked him directly, he informed me that his love for football led him to college. So, it was almost an accident that led him to his chosen career. It was not however, an accident that allowed him to succeed and excel. He has always demonstrated a strong determination to excel. Whatever he did, he did it with a passion.

As we talked, my mind drifted back many years to our time as teenagers, when the weightlifting fad caught on in the neighborhood. Most of us lifted weights until we were tired, but Rodney lifted them until I thought he was going to hurt himself. I used to have to get tired for him, because it didn't seem like he had sense enough to.

You see, when he worked out, he thought of the goal of playing football; when I worked out, my goal was to get finished and rest. So, it doesn't matter what your circumstances are. If you don't possess the proper attitude, if you don't continue to learn, if you are not motivated, if you don't persist, you won't develop into the person you are capable of becoming.

In many cases, the story would become stagnant at this point. Here we have a successful dentist who could now afford to coast through life, or could he? Dr. Foster wasn't about to let the cobwebs set in. He recognized, as few of us do, that there is a great big world out there, full of opportunities for those who choose a better life. He decided to start Foster Enterprises.

Foster Enterprises is involved in a concept called network marketing, a concept which provides an opportunity for a better lifestyle by building a business and saving money on consumption. After eight years of higher education, leading to a career in dentistry, after many additional hours of training required to maintain and improve his skills in dentistry, after many years of experience and growth, Dr. Foster had the vision to see even more opportunity, the attitude to achieve, and the motivation to persist.

To complete this chapter, I decided to attend an opportunity meeting with Dr. Foster. I found over 200 people gathered at a hotel meeting room just outside Cleveland to hear Marshall Johnson, a former football player for the Baltimore Colts. Marshall was in town to speak on the network marketing opportunity, and what the crowd size told me was that there was plenty of need and desire out there.

Experience told me that most of them would not change their lifestyles measurably. Not because the opportunity was missing, but because the difference in the winners and losers in life is the action they take or fail to take in their own behalf. I repeat, the difference in the winners and losers in life is the action they take or fail to take in their own behalf.

As good as Marshall Johnson was, and he was good, as good as network marketing is, there are going to be some individuals that go half-stepping into the plan, naked of the tools required to succeed, missing the mindset required to make the sacrifices necessary to succeed in network marketing or any other business.

In this book I attempt to provide you with those attributes you need to develop and improve. Those include, but are not limited to, attitude, motivation and persistence. In this book I have provided some practical examples of where such attributes have been developed and applied, such as this story of Dr. Foster. Armed with the information in this book, a strong heart, and a made up mind, you are prepared to win not only the war, but most of the battles.

Les Brown Unlimited
Les Brown, *"Mamie Brown's Baby Boy"*

By now many readers know Les Brown's story. But for those who might not have been tuned in, or just as a refresher, here it is.

Les was an adopted child who was at one time judged to be educable mentally retarded. He received no formal education after high school, but has achieved fame as a disc jockey, a member of the Ohio State Legislature, and most recently as an internationally known speaker and trainer. Despite his fame, he communicates with everyone with whom he has contact in a friendly and direct manner.

Les is used by many Fortune 500 companies for sales seminars, at meetings regarding company downsizing, and other times which require that a positive mental attitude be stressed.

I had the pleasure of being in an audience that Les addressed on two occasions prior to 1994. At one session, Les had students from his two day workshop speak to the audience. It was apparent that his enthusiasm as a speaker is contagious. It served as a reminder that the primary reason many fail to achieve is not from lack of ability, but rather lack of training, education, nurturing, and persistence.

His topics and his approach are upbeat, citing positive examples, and admitting but downplaying the effect of *"Murphy's Law"* on the outcome of an individual's achievements. Everywhere Les goes that I know of, he is very well received.

While I was preparing this book for publication, I attended a two and one-half day workshop conducted by Les, and the experience was mind-boggling. That workshop experience, and having the good fortune to meet and talk with Les on two other occasions shortly after the workshop has left me ecstatic. As this book goes to print, I am in the process of organizing interested speakers from that workshop for the purposes of continued personal and professional growth.

Maxima Corporation
Joshua Smith

Joshua Smith is one of those people you just have to meet and talk to, if you are to fully appreciate this financial and political giant. He is founder and chief executive officer of a sixteen-year old company which grossed over $58,000,000 in 1989 and was appointed by former President Bush to head the Commission on Minority Business.

Joshua heads Maxima Corporation, listed number nine in 1989 in the ***Black Enterprise*** Top 100 Industrial/Service Companies. Maxima is in the business of systems engineering and computer management, and is headquartered in Rockville, Maryland.

The good part is yet to come. With these credentials, you would almost expect to find a high, mighty, mostly unreachable individual. The fact is, Joshua Smith mixes easily with others who have not yet achieved such a high level of success. He gives freely of his time, energy, and expertise to those who are seeking to help themselves.

I have met Joshua on three occasions, and have benefited greatly from his seminars, from his expertise as a keynote speaker, and from his friendly and outgoing nature. Although I confess to knowing very little of his past, my personal knowledge of him and the public record agree that he represents a combination of personality and accomplishment that is a worthy goal for us all.

SuccessSource
George C. Fraser

I have sought in the preceding chapters to bring you those components necessary for your *'building block of success'*. I now offer you a brief story of a man who is making it happen, in Cleveland and across the nation.

George C. Fraser, Founder and President of SuccessSource is doing as the SuccessSource theme line suggests, *"Linking people and ideas."* The rebirth of Cleveland would not have been the same, nor would so many minorities have been involved, had it not been for things like *SuccessNet, SuccessMail and SuccessGuide*, all registered names of *SuccessSource*. I am not going to believe that I know them all, because as I write, you can be certain that George is thinking, and implementing and making things happen.

George's network of success has spread to at least ten cities nationwide and if I don't hurry and finish this book, he will have added ten more. Outwardly calm, quiet, personable and always looking unruffled, George has taken what I will refer to as his *success components* and created an informal network of entrepreneurs, employees and businesspeople that could change the economic balance in this country. Merely dropping George a business card gets you into *SuccessGuide*, a valuable book described by George as *"the road map for Black professionals and entrepreneurs."* George enabled Black people to network in a simple but overlooked way and the short term effect was more viable businesses and improved selection and service for the consumer.

The long term effects baffle the imagination, because anyone who knows George, knows that he has only just begun. Looking beneath the surface of short term effects and beyond the rewards of tangible business growth, I feel comfortable and pleased that George has really empowered and involved Black people as they must be empowered and involved as America moves into the 21st century.

By giving Black Americans more options, by improving their economic clout, by making them aware of their abilities, George's long term effects defy measurement. What he has begun will have a ripple effect throughout the nation and the world. That ripple could become a wave as future generations reap the possibilities that he has helped to create. All of America needs to understand that empowered people, productive people, motivated people are a prerequisite to the survival of this nation. Viable Black businesses can turn ghettos into gold mines and change welfare to workfare.

Let there be no mistake about it, the issues we face transcend race and encompass economics. America cannot afford unmotivated people and untapped resources, so the benefactors of the *success components* go far beyond the physical limits of the ghetto and far beyond the mental barriers of race.

When I asked for a fax of George Fraser's bio, I had no idea that the fax machine would run out of paper. People standing nearby must have thought I was receiving an encyclopedia. I will share just a bit of George's bio, since Millicent Fraser was kind enough to send it to me. It really does belong in a LARGE encyclopedia.

George is a graduate of the Amos Tuck School of Business at Dartmouth College and New York University, George's impressive work experience includes being a marketing manager for Procter & Gamble and director of marketing and communications at United Way. He has worked for Ford Motor Company and been a radio host on a nationally syndicated daily mini-series.

George's major accomplishments and awards fill more than a full typewritten page. His community service speaks well for his concern, and happily for me, it reinforces my firm belief of the teaching and growing power inherent in community involvement.

One of George's speeches was selected for reprint by the prestigious *Vital Speeches of the Day*, and circulated nationally. He appeared on the July 1994 cover of *Black Enterprise Magazine* and was named *Black America's #1 Networker*. His accolades simply will not fit into the space I have allotted in this book, but fear not, George recently released his own book, *SUCCESS RUNS IN OUR RACE*.

Wilco Information Management
Kenneth Wilson

Often in describing a rare event, we use the term *'once in a blue moon'*. Kenneth (Ken) Wilson is the type of individual you meet *'once in a blue moon'*. I met Ken in the early 1980's at a class in IDMS, a database management system used by many companies in their computer processing. Ken impressed me as friendly, but quiet.

I really got to know him best as the President of the Cleveland chapter of Black Data Processing Associates, a position he held for five years. During those five years, the Cleveland chapter grew and developed into a recognized front runner in what I've previously described as a quality organization. During his leadership, the Cleveland chapter received national recognition in several areas, and was named Chapter of The Year by the national organization on more than one occasion during those five years.

You might wonder what all this has to do with Wilco Information Management, an information processing consulting firm which Ken founded in 1984. The fact is that Ken brought to Wilco what he brought to BDPA -- quiet, unassuming, professional, and effective leadership.

Ken's education, training, and background include general business management, project management, consulting and information systems development activities. Ken holds a Bachelors degree in Mathematics, and has completed finance, accounting and marketing courses toward an MBA degree. He has authored articles and presented seminars on the topic of computer data management.

Ken holds the Certificate in Data Processing (CDP) designation, and in addition to his membership in BDPA, he holds membership in the Association for Computer Machinery (ACM) and the Independent Computer Consultants Association (ICCA).

In his spare time Ken serves as a Little League baseball coach, works with the Boy Scouts, is in the Career Beginnings mentorship program, and is an active church member. In addition to being an avid jogger, Ken enjoys participating and watching many other sports. He also does a little piano playing, and enjoys many types of music and gardening.

Ken and his lovely wife Deborah also have the challenge of raising two children, Kevin and Leslie. My next book may be a mystery novel entitled _"When Does Ken Wilson Sleep?"_

Having simultaneously built a business, provided leadership for an organization that is a winner among winners, started a family, continued an education, and remained sane, should be proof of the qualities Ken exhibits, and a reason to inquire into the services of WILCO, should you or your organization be in the market for computer services. For all readers, Ken's story should be a source of motivation for achievement and excellence, and proof that it can be done with a disposition the world can live with.

In reviewing biographical information that I squeezed out of Ken, I was impressed by the following quotes;

"A key turning point in my career was when I joined BDPA. Prior to my joining, I had not accepted full responsibility for my career not progressing as rapidly as I'd wanted it to. Nor had I learned to properly respond to the subtle discrimination that was also helping stagnate my career. Although WILCO has been somewhat successful during its first six years, I envision building a new organization which will serve as a model of how American companies should be run to compete internationally."

In only four sentences, we see a testament to growth, a testament to education, the learning of techniques to counter the ever present challenges of the marketplace, an acknowledgment of success, and the vision for a greater future. All this from a man who has yet to reach forty-five years of age.

By the way, Ken's interpretation of _"somewhat successful"_ includes letters of appreciation from corporate clients such as Argo-Tech Corporation, Progressive Companies, Dow Chemical U.S.A., General Electric Credit Corporation, and Anacomp Inc, among others.

Ken Wilson surely exemplifies what I have sought to address in this book, and I am proud to have brought you this example of what you too can achieve.

Examples Of Excellence
Looking Into The Mirror And At The
1994 BDPA Conference Attendees

"The positive and involved mind is certainly one of the mechanisms that energizes and empowers us."

Identifying tomorrow's winners is not an easy task. We have a potential pool of applicants much larger than you might imagine. What the future will bring depends on a complex combination of factors for which there is no mathematical formula.

What I do feel safe in predicting is that those who are reading these words or those who listen to the sound of my voice have a better than average chance of being tomorrow's winners. It has little to do with what I have to offer, but much to do with the audience's self-concept and commitment to excellence. Those people that attended my August, 1994 workshop at the BDPA National Conference are examples of tomorrow's winners.

It is from my audience that I draw the strength to continue. Rather than me empowering the audience, they, in fact, empower me. As I will allude to again later, you cannot teach without learning. The positive and involved mind is certainly one of the mechanisms that energizes and empowers us.

My thanks to the members of the 1994 BDPA workshop includes dedicating part of this chapter to their dreams. I also have a selfish motive for doing this. I truly believe that seated in my audience that day were the winners of the future. When they make their footprints in the sands of time, I want it known that I was associated with them. I want it to be assumed that I played a small part in their journey of success.

On August 19, 1994 these individuals took a giant step toward greatness by opening their minds to the message and their hearts to the possibilities. I urge you to do likewise by carefully considering what you might have in common with these individuals.

Angela Goode
Wilmington, Delaware

Angela works for Dupont as team leader of the Electronic Messaging Support Group. She has a Bachelor of Science degree in accounting from Hampton University. This former high school valedictorian loves to read, meet new people, do one-on-one training, listen to music and encourage and support others. She also enjoys sightseeing of historic sites, particularly African-American museums. Sewing, water aerobics, touring gardens, attending cultural events, plays, outside concerts are also on her *list of things to do.*

Angela's ambitions include possibly becoming a travel planner, trainer, catalog model or writer. When asked to share deeper feelings, Angela responded with

"God grant me the serenity. . . to accept the things I cannot change, courage to change the things I can, and the wisdom to know the difference. Living one day at a time enjoying one moment at a time, accepting hardship as the pathway to peace. . .That I may be reasonably happy in this life and supremely happy with him forever in the next. "

Angela is happily married to Randy Goode and they have three children, Travis, Tiara and Ariana, ages 10, 4 and 3. A careful look at Angela's activities shows a curiosity for learning and a zest for living. These two things will serve her well on her journey of success.

Roger Mabin
Southfield, Michigan

With 26 years in data processing you might think Roger Mabin would be getting ready to relax and coast into retirement. With a vision typical of successful people, he has only begun to show the world what he is made of. Roger holds a Bachelor of

Science in chemistry, he has done graduate work in computer science and is currently working toward an MBA.

Roger has discovered personal satisfaction in the work of the ministry and expects to be a full-time minister within two years. Looking at his competence in such diverse areas, hints that Roger Mabin will be a great asset to the ministry, and that his success will be reflected in those whose lives he will touch.

Robert Smokey Montgomery
Jamaica Plain, Massachusetts

A native of Roxbury, Massachusetts, Robert's pursuit of excellence and community involvement have resulted in many accolades. His Bachelor of Science in electrical engineering technology from Northeastern University and Graduate Certificate in applied sciences from Harvard only begins to tell the story.

Robert is a software engineer for Lotus Development Corporation. In 1986 he received the Black Achievers Award from Wang Laboratory. He is a board member and youth mentor with INROADS of Central New England. Robert is the founder of the Community Outreach Committee for Non-Profit Organizations.

With such an impressively list of accomplishments, and I didn't include them all, you might suspect that Robert has not yet fulfilled all his dreams. He plans to pursue his passions and help others to identify and pursue their passions in life. Robert's life certainly demonstrates a rigorous adherence to the success principles.

Peggy Norman
Westchester, Illinois

Peggy Norman's Bachelor of Arts from DePaul University and Master of Science in Management only begin to tell the story of her educational background. Peggy has traveled extensively to Africa, the Far East, Australia, Europe and South America. She certainly has extensive knowledge and understanding of the world's people and cultures. With that knowledge goes the sharing with those living outside the United States. One of the biggest challenges facing Americans is to understand and accept the culture of others. The world market offers opportunity and challenge and Peggy has valuable knowledge that American citizens and American companies need.

Peggy retired from Consolidated Edison in early 1994. Although she has expressed no immediate plans to capitalize on her asset, she is not idle. When Peggy is not traveling, she fills in the gaps of time as a real estate representative. Strategically positioned with knowledge of sales and international customs and people, Peggy Norman certainly has the potential for a future just as successful as her past.

Blanche Williams
Dayton, Ohio

Blanche Williams has been *"beating the odds"* for a long time. She describes the challenges she has faced as *"a refrigerator on her back."* Blanche recognizes that a low-income family background, being one of eight siblings and being a divorced mother of two, can qualify as negative mental conditioning. She also shared the challenges of a daughter who is a kidney transplant recipient.

As though she didn't have enough challenges, Blanche also had the misfortune of having an eighth grade teacher who advised her against taking algebra or any college prep courses. Her teacher reasoned that she wouldn't be able to afford it anyway.

Unshaken by circumstances that would have caused many to give up, Blanche presently works as a systems consultant and is returning to college in the fall of 1994. She would like to eventually go into the field of education, using her computer knowledge, her love of learning and teaching, and her love of children to encourage young people to identify their individual gifts and talents and develop into happy and productive adults.

Blanche stated that if she isn't able to get *"the refrigerator off her back"* she will still work toward her goals and not use her situation as an excuse to be a quitter.

Others On The Move
The New Generation of Entrepreneurs
and Their Success Summaries

There is a generation of Americans who have witnessed and been a part of the *"new industrial revolution"*. It is a revolution that has resulted in American jobs going South to Mexico, North to Canada, West to the Orient and East to Europe. It is a revolution that has touched the entire working class of this nation either physically or mentally.

Those who have not lost a job may have been downgraded. Those who have escaped downgrading may have had a reduction in pay or benefits. Those who still earn the same pay often do not have the luxury of changing jobs, for they are prisoners of their own temporary affluence, worrying about that fateful tap on the shoulder. Anyone not in one of those categories is either lucky or naive.

All these items fall into the category of that inevitable thing we call CHANGE. Change doesn't have to be good, or bad, or fair, or reasonable, it's just change.

Survival and success require adaptability, vision and courage. As corporate America replaces the soothing effects of retirement *security* with the harsh reality of *get old and get out*, visionary people of all ages are turning to entrepreneurship as a viable alternative or additional means of security.

Several of these individuals are included in the remainder of this chapter. My hope is that their stories will encourage you to consider your particular situation. My hope is that if you dream of business ownership, that you will find an example that inspires you to move forward.

Eleanor Askew
LMT Massotherapist

Eleanor decided that she had the motivation and persistence to go beyond the limits of what corporate America had to offer.

With many working years remaining, Eleanor embarked on a second career as a licensed massotherapist. She specializes in Professional Therapeutic Massages.

Clifford Anderson
Anderson Builders

Specializing in quality home and office construction, Cliff is experienced, dependable, quiet and unassuming, He consistently delivers a product and a service that keeps his customers happy and referrals coming in.

Connie Atkins
Atkins Professional Advantage (APA)

A businesswoman since 1982, Connie brings to her clients uncompromising professionalism. Her wealth of business knowledge, attention to detail and dedication to quality work keeps her customers coming back for more. APA trains employees how to work smarter, and Connie's efforts are well recognized by the Cleveland business community.

Although her corporate accounts keep her extremely busy, Connie finds the time to promote the networking of small business owners through the Cleveland Business Consortium. Not only does she exhibit those qualities necessary for successful business ownership, but she enjoys giving something back through support of the consortium and other civic activities.

Ors Banhidy
JSS Computer Systems

Being exceptionally competent and personable with the ability to lead and teach allowed Ors to establish JSS Computer Systems. Downsizing and outsourcing jeopardized his career, but being prepared, he was able to exercise options not available to those who are the victims of complacency.

Barry Bennett and Sandie Bennett
Bennett Barber Shop and Bennett Bookkeeping & Tax Service

This couple had a double barreled response to the limits corporate America would have placed on their vision. In the business of hair cutting and styling, Barry has a large and loyal following because of his dependability and commitment to quality service. Sandie has put her experience working for a major utility company, and her work as an independent consultant and professional tax training to excellent use.

Ronald Berhent
Berhent Financial Services

Competent, professional and supportive are some of the ways you could describe Ron Berhent, a *"victim"* of corporate downsizing. Victim is in quotes because Ron prepared himself for life after corporate America.

An accountant who decided not to wait for the ax, Ron became an *enrolled agent* and is qualified to represent clients before the Internal Revenue Service, if required. He is also an *accredited tax adviser*, certified by the Accreditation Council for Accountancy and Taxation (ACAT). Ron performs tax, accounting and consulting services for individuals and small businesses. While corporate America sharpened the ax, Ron sharpened his skills and the result was not a victim, but a winner.

Ralph Burton
Burton & Associates

Extremely professional and customer oriented, Ralph has successfully established himself in the highly competitive insurance business as a force to be reckoned with.

He commitment to quality customer service has earned him the nickname of *The Master*. Ralph trains and has business relationships with several insurance agents. He demonstrates an upward mobility that has him "aiming for the moon."

Vernest Dickson
Independent Mary Kay Consultant

Hard working, talented, personable and qualified in the field of accounting, Vernest is a person you might think would have become complacent. Wise beyond her years, Vernest is supplementing her income and her vision as a Mary Kay consultant.

As the busy mother of a beautiful daughter, Shandora, Vernest demonstrates that you can balance career and family and still work on your dreams.

Doris Edwards
H & S Gallery

Twenty-six years in corporate America did not provide for Doris Edwards the degree of independence and freedom she desired. Working harder now than she ever has, Doris has an expanded degree of control and does not miss the confinement she experienced working for someone else.

Doris is the owner of H & S Gallery, specializing in Black art and custom framing. Doris recently added open and limited edition prints and collectibles to her growing variety of quality products.

Antoinette Francis
Independent Real Estate Representative

A highly-qualified, competent and dependable accountant, Antoinette used her knowledge of numbers and her love for people to launch a real estate career. She saw beyond the *'glass ceiling'* corporate America had placed above her.

Eloise Henry
Independent Mary Kay Consultant

This educator who is well-respected by students, teachers and administrators, is also a successful Mary Kay Consultant.

Eloise balances the challenges of being a wife and mother remarkably well and always has a kind word for those whose lives she touches.

James Jackson Jr. and Tony Jackson
Independent Representatives - Quorum, International

From opposite sides of the country, these quiet and easy going brothers have entered the field of network marketing as independent representatives with Quorum, International.

Their market focuses on the fast growing and socially rewarding field of security devices. Both still employed, they have the foresight and vision that they can go beyond their present limits.

Norman Mays
N.R. Mays Associates

Norman has distinguished himself in several areas, including that of organizer, public speaker, and a specialist in information systems security. Norman is currently marketing computerized educational material which focuses on Black achievement, including African and American History.

Norman has made good use of his knowledge of information systems and marketing to perform the socially responsible task of motivating Black Americans.

Johnnie McAnulty
Goddess Hair Design

Being a beautician can be rewarding, not only in income, but in the people you meet and become associated with. Johnnie McAnulty saw beyond those rewards. She reasoned that if she could do it for someone else, that she could do it even better for herself.

Certainly there were risks involved, but Johnnie had a vision that went beyond the minefield of risks, and into the promise land of rewards.

When she opened Goddess, her reputation of being a quality person really became apparent. Even though she did not try to *hire away* anyone from her former employer, half of her former co-workers left and joined the Goddess staff.

Tangy Poindexter
Executive Nails by Tangy

Being talented and employable did not deter Tangy from realizing her dream of business ownership. Tangy chose the rewards of satisfaction, over the false security of corporate America.

Because of her commitment to quality service, after only a short time in the business, she has to turn some new customers away.

Ken Raines
Good News Family Bookstore

Religious and practical, Ken Raines combines faith, knowledge, good business sense and social responsibility in the operation of his bookstore. The store specializes in religious and motivational books, tapes and other products.

Carol and Sonny Richards
Catering By Carol

True entrepreneurial genius might describe Carol and Sonny. Using innovative ideas such as cooking everything in your home for your special celebration, Sonny and Carol are well known for their quality products and services, which they always deliver with a smile.

Carol and Sonny also are the exclusive caterers for a popular Bedford Heights, Ohio location.

Greg Smith

"Customer service oriented" could be Greg's middle name. Greg's reputation for quality drapery installation is well known by those fortunate enough to have used his services.

Greg's workmanship and sense of responsibility have resulted in him doing subcontract work for major chain stores in the northeast Ohio area.

Harry & Mary Sykes
Professional Caterers and Party Planners

Professional Caterers and Party Planners is growing so fast that it depletes my energy just keeping up with their progress. The engineer on this *train ride to success* is Harry, who has years of experience in the catering and food business and a total commitment to quality. Harry's meticulous attention to food taste and appearance is a trademark. Mary is the conductor that keeps Harry from jumping the tracks due to excess speed.

Together they operate the business which currently has several food contracts, including one across the street from Cleveland's new Gateway Complex.

Joseph Taylor
Taylor Electrical, Inc.

Over twenty-five years in corporate America taught Joseph Taylor that he is undoubtedly qualified to own and operate his own business.

Committed and steady as a rock, twice during those twenty-five years Joe became one of the many victims of downsizing or rightsizing or whatever the current name is for the disruption of lives.

Spurred on by his wife June, Joe has taken his years of electronics and electrical background and parlayed it into a successful business, providing both commercial and residential service.

Cornelius Turner
C. Turner Plumbing Company

In this time of high-priced and often shoddy workmanship, Cornelius Turner is a blessing. His total customer focus creates a demand that he cannot keep up with. He somehow has the ability to respond to emergencies, and he builds a customer relationship that creates a high comfort level.

Turner consistently demonstrates a pride in workmanship that builds a solid and loyal customer base.

Gordon Weston
Gordon Weston Insurance Company

Gordon Weston, President of Gordon Weston Insurance, has survived and prospered in the competitive insurance industry for seven years. He offers his growing customer base their choice of a variety of fire, auto, life and health insurance.

Gordon's key to survival is personalized quality service. His biggest obstacle in providing life insurance is convincing people of the need to invest in their future. Gordon's advice to others entering the industry is to prepare to work long hours, be persistent and keep your word.

His adherence to sound business principles has resulted in as much as a 40% increase in a single year.

These Are Just A Few of Many

The people I have written about are representative of that entrepreneurial spirit that has engulfed America. They are representative of people who refuse to let life dictate their circumstances.

These are just a few of the people who have decided that they are not going to accept the status quo as an immobile object. They have decided that there is something inside them that they can offer to the world. They have visions and dreams, and certainly sometimes they have setbacks.

Over the years, I have dealt with perhaps thousands of business owners and I offer my apologies to those who were not mentioned. My purpose here is to let the reader, the potential business owner, understand that they are not alone. I also needed to provide graphic examples of average people that went beyond average by reaching for some of the values I have written about in this book.

Profiles of Inspiration

Mr. Bertram Gardner
Friend, Mentor and Role Model

Having known Bertram Gardner for over thirty years can be compared to having your own personal advisor available when you need them. Sometimes after not talking to Bert for months, I run into a situation that I can't handle, pick up the phone, and a very busy but undaunted Bert Gardner either answers or calls back very soon.

A well known, highly respected and very much liked Bert has served in such capacities as Director of the Glenville YM-YWCA, Community Relations Director for the City of Cleveland and Vice President of Urban Affairs at Cleveland Trust Bank. Bert has served on numerous corporate boards and in a variety of community service organizations.

I have neither the time, the patience, or enough room in this book to mention all the good things I know about Bert. I just want you to know that without Bert Gardner, I probably would not have written *Success Is You*. One secret of the universe that I will never know, is whether the job Bert Gardner gave me at the YM-YWCA in 1964 meant the difference between me being a major contributor or a minor statistic. Thanks again Bert.

John Fitzgerald Kennedy
The 35th President of The United States

The *'1000 Days'* of John F. Kennedy's administration were some of the most significant days of my life. His Presidency found itself deeply involved in major issues of the twentieth century, namely civil rights, the Communist threat and organized crime.

That would have been enough, but the issues were magnified and intensified because of several personal factors. For most of the Kennedy years, I was in the U.S. Army. I was stationed in Georgia during the Bay of Pigs invasion and in Germany during the Cuban Missile Crisis. My upbringing, my sense of responsibility and my belief in American principles made me proud and ready.

Kennedy's youth, his style and his rhetoric lent to me a sense of belonging.   The President who was there as I experienced the transformation from the teen years to adulthood, was himself youthful, vigorous and idealistic.

History found him as a key player in the struggle for civil rights, an issue that was to be the culmination of 400 years of neglect and mistreatment. As Governors and Presidents squared off, my faith in the American way was usually reinforced by the results.

Engraved in my mind is the conversation between a Governor and the commander of the National Guard Unit activated to enforce segregation. After the National Guard was placed under federal control, the commander approached the Governor, saluted and officially stated, *"Sir, I regret to inform you that the Guard has been federalized."* The Commander was in favor of segregation, but his commitment was to the due process of law.   His commitment was to his duty, so he performed that duty and yielded to that which was inevitable.

Being proud to be an American was easy during times like that. Imagine my shock on November 22, 1963, when a President fell victim to an assassin's bullet and a nation grieved. Almost as unbelievable as the events in Dallas that day was the cheering of co-workers who heard the news.

Yes, there are among us those who cheered the death of a father, husband and world leader, just because they disagreed with him. Just to make sure I took it personally, one lady asked me *"what are you people going to do now?"* I thought that as Shipping and Receiving Clerk, I would keep moving boxes; that was my job. Of course, the President had only been doing his job and that didn't seem to affect his tormentors.

I just want those people who worked with me in that small west side Cleveland manufacturing plant to know that November 22, 1963 has not been forgotten.   If John F. Kennedy, or Martin Luther King, Jr., or the four young girls in Birmingham, or the three civil rights workers in Mississippi died so that I might succeed, then consider that the mission has been accomplished.

So what does all this have to do with you? The message is that you probably won't have to die to succeed. You just have to live for yourself. So by contrast, your task is simple.

Dr. Martin Luther King, Jr.
Civil Rights Leader

In December of 1992 I was honored to be asked to write the opening remarks for a program to honor Dr. Martin Luther King, Jr. to be presented at Stouffer's Tower City Center in Downtown Cleveland. To be given such an honor was an appropriate challenge along my route to success. Following is the complete text of those remarks.

As we celebrate the life of Dr. Martin Luther King, Jr., we celebrate a true champion of justice and equality. Dr. King attempted to cure the disease of racism. He challenged the widespread plague of poverty, and echoed an unpopular stand against an unjust war. He brought to the forefront conditions unfit for humankind.

It was Dr. King's commitment to basic human ideals that allowed him to stand with the strength of David against the Goliath system of segregation. It was his belief that second class citizenship had no rightful place in the richest country in the world. It was a belief that propelled this nation into the largest movement for equality the world has ever known. It was his politically unpopular but morally correct position against the Viet Nam war that established the birth of a movement for peace.

Through Dr. King's vision, through his leadership, through his capacity to endure pain and suffering, he brought to the world the elusive commodity of hope. Thirty years later, that commodity is still in short supply.

Thirty years later, we have an increase not only in poverty of material things; but more regrettably, in poverty of the mind and poverty of spirit. Thirty years later, racism still wears the mask of hate in the form of burning crosses and videotaped beatings. Today, racism has an expanded wardrobe. Today racism also wears the disguise of negative mental conditioning.

Thirty years later, there is war not only in far away lands, but in our own backyard. The degenerative diseases of abuse, neglect, broken families and broken promises have created a grim prognosis.

The nature of our illness requires more than the antibiotic of a new plan or the sedating effect of new leadership. We must all become active players in this game called life.

As Dr. King did, we must all become drum majors for justice. As Dr. King did, we must become visionary in our thoughts. We must establish a strong belief system, make morally correct decisions and maintain a strong commitment.

Dr. King sat in jail so we could sit in the classroom. Drum Majors for Justice have different tunes to play, they have different orchestras to direct.   Whatever your talents and abilities might be, you have a place in the greatest show on earth, the uplifting of Black Americans.

The sweetest music to Dr. King's ears would be a symphony of Black Americans. A symphony having goals higher than the best soprano, their minds fine tuned like quality instruments. A symphony of Black Americans displaying the mental keenness of the band director and the strength of a base drummer, all marching to the rhythm of success.

Dr. Robert L. Lawson
Speaker, Trainer, Author, Administrator, Friend and Role Model

I met Dr. Robert Lawson, Bob as he insists I call him, at a meeting of the Ohio Speakers Forum (OSF). OSF is the Ohio Chapter of the National Speakers Association (NSA). I can remember wondering if membership in the two organizations could possibly be worth the price. My meeting Bob answered the question quickly and without reservation.   There is something that happens to you when you are around positive people that causes you to transcend mediocrity. It adds a value to your person that money cannot purchase.

A friendly and open individual, Bob has a reserved demeanor that fails to suggest how competent he really is. After knowing him a short time, I found that Cuyahoga Community College in Cleveland had contracted with Bob to have him present a workshop called *Destined For Greatness*.

I attended the workshop to see what I could learn, to find out what others in the field were doing. I was astounded! From the moment Bob opened his mouth for a solid hour he had his audience on the edge of their chairs. I was afraid to stop listening to him, afraid that I would miss the most important moment of my life. His audience was so warmed up that he had to break after an hour so no one would catch on fire.

That was only part of the good news. Bob told me that he would introduce me to his publisher, Matt Krise of Kendall-Hunt Publishing Company, and he did. Bob told me he would give me the names of contacts that might help me secure speaking engagements, and he did. Bob told me that he was interested in doing a workshop and allowing me to be a part of it to get more local exposure, and the workshop has been planned.

Everything that Bob has promised, he has delivered. I get excited just thinking about working with an individual of his caliber who can and will take the time and effort to share his success. Bob has a book out now entitled *Destined For Greatness*. I would strongly suggest that you add a copy to your personal development library.

Aleta Mays
Author, Friend and Mentor

It is difficult to impress me so much with phone calls that you find a place in this book under *Profiles of Greatness*. Aleta Mays is just that impressive. As I prepare this page, I have yet to meet Aleta. In the several months since we were put in contact by Bob Lawson, Aleta has shared ideas and inspiration. She has marketed my ideas, promoted my vision, passed out my literature and *dropped* my name in the presence of people who may be willing to open doors to speaking opportunities.

Aleta demonstrates with her heart what many of us profess with our mouths. She takes the concept of networking seriously and she takes it to a new level, providing opportunity and hope to those who have chosen to make a difference. In a soon to be released book entitled **_One Monkey Don't Stop No Show_**, I'm certain Aleta will share her success principles. I plan to be one of the first to learn more about this inspiring lady.

The Extended Family
Success Multiplied

"Sherbia Jones and Ruth Mitchell, cousins that I didn't know before our reunions started, were instrumental in booking my first major speaking engagement."

In the early 1970's, a very close first cousin, Synnia Solomon had the idea to start a family reunion. She did a lot of research, talking and convincing to bring together relatives of several generations. Fate dictated that Synnia would not live to see the first reunion, something she had worked so very hard for. Her untimely and unfortunate passing brought together other family members, including myself, to continue the effort she had begun.

1974 began the first of what has now become twenty-one consecutive annual reunions. Our reunions have taken place in Ohio, Michigan, New York State, North Carolina, Georgia and even in Windsor, Ontario.

I have watched our family mature and grow together. What inspires me is the variety of interests and talents the family has. Alone we might appear insignificant in the greater scheme of things, but get us together and there are myths to be shattered and records to be broken. Whenever families or groups of people get together and focus on positive things, miracles begin to happen.

Although special, our family is not unique. I recall having the opportunity to speak at the reunion of our friends Ralph and Sherryl Burton. When I heard the singing in that family, when I witnessed young Black males, speaking eloquently and professing love and commitment without reservation, I was almost afraid to speak, I didn't think they needed a positive message. There is so much latent talent and untapped power in our families that I am surprised over and over again. It simply defies the imagination.

In 1984, my sister Jean produced a family cookbook that she still gets requests for. That same year, I started a scholarship fund to recognize and encourage educational excellence. Named after Synnia, the scholarship recognizes our young family members for their educational achievements. We have excellent singers, dancers, a former author, a nationally known playwright, bank officials, business owners, and a variety of positive role models.

I have been inspired by watching borderline teens gravitate toward excellence when exposed to positive role models within the family. I am thrilled by how young people will grab a microphone and express themselves in a positive way and not be ashamed. At forty years of age, had you approached me with a microphone, I would have treated it like a live stick of dynamite. I would have shouted "GET THAT THING AWAY FROM ME!"

It was a first cousin, Margaret Ford-Taylor that for many years encouraged me to develop my writing and speaking skills. Sherbia Jones and Ruth Mitchell, cousins that I didn't know before our reunions started, were instrumental in booking my first major speaking engagement.

They risked their own reputation by speaking confidently in my behalf, at a time when I seriously doubted myself. They demonstrated the type of support that even money cannot purchase.

There is so much potential available from the synergism created at family gatherings that I urge you to take the time and effort to attend them. If you don't have one, start one. The processes and challenges you will go through are character building and provide a forum for building skills such as negotiation, a requirement when dealing with hotels and planning functions.

The end result is very rewarding, but I simply do not have the space to go into detail in this book. Your personal and professional life can grow immensely from becoming a part of an extended family. If you have very few, or even no family members, hook on to a friend's family. Some of our most faithful attendees year after year, are not family members, but good friends. It doesn't matter to them or anyone else, it is about people sharing and caring and growing together.

In The Presence of Greatness
And You Probably Don't Even Know It

"Search the world if you must for your Acres of Diamonds, but only after you check your own back yard."

In the book *Acres of Diamonds*, Russell Conwell writes of a rich man, Ali Hafed, who in search of more riches, loses everything including his life. The irony is that the diamonds Hafed sought, were on the land he left behind. His riches were right beneath his nose, and he lost everything searching the world for them.

Sometimes the riches of talent and excellence are blossoming nearby, and yet we search far and wide looking for them. As I was completing this book, papers flying and midnight oil burning, I overheard my wife Dianne talking to a friend on the phone. Fortunately I paused in my hectic pace long enough to realize that the conversation was about Jamie, the ten year old daughter of Joseph (Joe) and June Taylor, long time friends of ours.

Jamie had just won another award in golf. Yes *golf*, something many of us do for relaxation, something that has other possibilities. It is a sport that has the potential of handsome rewards such as building character and earning scholarships. It is an area often overlooked by blacks simply because our present and future tends to be a mirror of our past.

The last time I had seen Jamie was when Dianne and I attended a Student of The Year program at Jamie's school. Jamie, an excellent student, was a finalist in the competition. I started thinking about how Jamie, also an excellent athlete, might be an ideal role model in this book.

A few of Jamie's other accomplishments include being Vice President of Student Council and Captain of the Safety Patrol. Her school memberships include the Broadcaster's Club, Literature Club, Chorus and Cheerleading Squad. She is an active member of Unity Church, a member of the Tennis Program, the Siemma Science Program and others. As a girl scout, Jamie has achieved Cadette status.

Jamie's older brother Christopher (Chris) is already making his mark at the young age of fifteen. His musical ability includes singing and playing the saxophone. A member of the Warrensville Heights Marching and Concert Bands, Chris also plays basketball, tennis, golf and is a member of the Boy Scouts.

Chris keeps education in its proper place by maintaining a highly respectable 3.4 grade point average on a 4.0 point scale. Chris takes all honors classes and has been in a summer engineering program and the Readers Club. In his spare time, he works with his father and has learned to repair electrical appliance circuits.

What a coincidence I thought, both children in one family who represent the vision and principles of _Success Is You_. Two children in one family who do what they do so well and so quietly, that it had become easy not to notice them. What a stroke of luck for the parents, I reasoned.

Then it finally registered, my brain finally kicked into gear. It wasn't a stroke of luck, but it was years of excellence by example. Here was a family that we had known for years, an ideal family to represent _Success Is You_. I had become so accustomed to the entire Taylor family being examples of success, that I had begun to take them for granted. In my frantic efforts to find that which was in my own backyard, I nearly became the modern day Ali Hafed, I nearly lost my _Acres of Diamonds_ for purposes of completing this book.

Joe and June Taylor established standards of excellence not by edict, but by example. They did it not by casting their children into learning and growing situations, but by accompanying them into such situations. They not only told their children how to be good community citizens, they showed them.

Joe is a business owner and Vice President of the Warrensville Heights, Ohio Optimist Club. A member of Excelsior Lodge #11, Joe is also a member of the City Planning Commission and a former school board member. He is involved in more than a half dozen community organizations. His numerous awards include the Picker Productivity Award in 1987 and being proclaimed *"Man Of The Year"* by Warrensville Heights in 1992.

June Taylor has been with the East Cleveland School System for twenty years and is presently a counselor in that system. She served three years as Assistant Director in the Career Beginnings Program at Case Western Reserve University.

Well known and respected in the community, June appeared on the television show *"Neighborhood"* in 1987 because of her expertise in mentoring, curriculum writing and people skills. Her long list of community involvement includes having served on the Board of Directors at Unity Church of Cleveland. June is presently the Youth Education Director for Unity Church of Cleveland, and the Scholarship Chairperson for Cleveland's East Technical High School *Class of '64 Association.* June is also a Merit Badge counselor for Boy Scout Troop 464 in Warrensville Heights.

My journey of success was made easier, because of referrals and continue interest that I received from Joe and June. The principles I bring you in this book are substantiated by the entire family. As you go about your journey of success, make a special effort to keep tuned in to those individuals who are making a difference. They probably won't be wearing t-shirts that identify them as the winners in life, but it will be worth the effort for you to identify them and identify with them. It is likely that you and they stand on common ground, and can be helpful to each other. Search the world if you must for your *Acres of Diamonds*, but only after you check your own back yard.

- Section 6 -
Giving and Receiving

Understanding Your Roots and Linking To Something Bigger Than Yourself
Karamu House As An Example

You Can't Teach Without Learning
Responsibility and Reward

Sharing Through Mentoring
Career Beginnings As An Example

Understanding Your Roots and Linking To Something Bigger Than Yourself
Karamu House As An Example

"Even in the darkest tunnel however, there often exists a ray of light, a reason for hope.   Enter Karamu House of greater Cleveland, the oldest Black performing and visual arts entity in the country."

Very often as we travel the road of success, it is easy to think that we are doing it alone. In my life there are many examples of people who appear to have a vision completely different than my own, yet their support has been crucial to my vision.

Sometimes we need to look around and see what others are doing. We could very often lend moral or financial support to another cause and find our own goals closer and more meaningful.

One of the positive things that comes to mind is supporting the arts. No matter what our racial or ethnic background, there is an important connection that needs to be strengthened and tapped into. Without knowledge of our past, the future is less focused.

I urge you whatever your racial and cultural heritage, to support the link to your past. Connection to the arts is constructive and educational, and a preferred alternative to entertainment which seeks to divide and depress.

Speaking and writing from a Black prospective comes naturally and therefore becomes necessary. I cannot and would not assume another identity to sell a book or an idea. I am who I am, and believing what I share, I believe the world is a better place because I am not like all the other people on earth.

You also bring a uniqueness that, when shared, can become an asset to those with whom you come in contact with. So if the Black experience is not your experience, bear with me as I share my identity.

In my roots reside a strength and a sense of direction that I could not have begged, borrowed, stolen or even purchased.

Therefore I am committed to the preservation and growth of the Black arts. What I offer to you, the reader, is *A Link To The Past, A Hope For The Future,* featuring **Karamu House of greater Cleveland.**

With a host of injustices ranging from the misdemeanor of benign neglect, to the capital crime of outright racism, most if not all industries at some time in history have contributed to the incarceration of the mind and spirit of Black America. The arts and entertainment industry is no exception.

Even that which America acknowledges we do well, they somehow have, by a variety of methods, denied Black America payment in full for the contributions that have been made to arts and entertainment. From the practice of casting white actors and actresses as Blacks, implying that a white person could act more like a Black person, than the Black person themselves; to the practice of substituting white pictures on the album covers of Black singers; the arts and entertainment industry has given true meaning to the term *"guilty as charged."*

Even in the darkest tunnel however, there often exists a ray of light, a reason for hope. Enter Karamu House of greater Cleveland, the oldest Black performing and visual arts entity in the country.

The good news is that Karamu has been a valued resource for over 75 years.   Through its doors have come such individuals as poet Langston Hughes, painter Hughie Lee Smith, composer Hale Smith, director Gilbert Moses, actors Robert Guillaume, Bill Cobbs, Minnie Gentry and Ron O'Neal.   In addition, the existence of Karamu House has provided a training arena for thousands of other professionals, onstage, backstage, directing, dancing, teaching, performing.

In the area of teaching the black experience, and providing a positive influence to audiences in Cleveland and the nation, Karamu House is rated second to none. Its contributions toward freeing and developing the black mind, and providing positive messages to build a bridge of understanding between people of all colors, should place its continued existence as a priority item not only within the Black community, but within the entire business and civic community of Cleveland.

The bad news is that Karamu House is operating on a *'shoestring budget'*, a budget not worthy of an institution so necessary to the survival of the Black race. While Cleveland's version of corporate America generously underwrites other arts institutions such as the Cleveland Playhouse, support of Karamu is not as easily forthcoming.

Before anyone takes to the streets with the arsenal of weapons ranging from the protest signs of the moderates, to the firebombs of the radicals, let us review our own pitiful support of such a fine institution. Karamu House is well situated within the Black community, on Cleveland's East Side, but it suffers from our lack of serious support.

The situation at Karamu is unlikely to change significantly in the near future, without the increased support of the Cleveland business community, and to the extent we can exert influence, we should work toward that end. That does not however, preclude you as an individual from the responsibility of doing your part to assure that Karamu remains viable. You don't have to bring bushels of money and dump it at the doorway, although no one will stop you if you are so inclined.

What many of us can do is to investigate the entertainment and other programs available at Karamu. It is all of high quality and low cost. It can provide refreshing selections on our menu of things to do.

If you get bored, contact Karamu House, and ask if you might lend your expertise to teach a class. If you don't have anything to teach, find out what they can teach you. If you don't like any of my ideas, call Karamu House, and ask them what they offer, ask them what they need. Be a part of the solution to what ails our community.

In support of my position, I quote the Cleveland Plain Dealer's Arts Review of September 16, 1990 where they state, *"The staff of Karamu, led by the intelligent and imaginative Margaret Ford-Taylor, plans an interesting anniversary season."* The article went on to state:

> *Although Karamu has pulled out of the massive deficits Ford-Taylor inherited in 1987 and its theater productions*

have been steadily improving, its financial situation is extremely fragile. Were it not for the intense loyalties of a small staff and volunteers, the institution would have closed.

Additional evidence of the seriousness of Karamu's financial situation, is provided by the fact that on October 10th of 1990, the Honorable Louis Stokes, Congressman from Ohio's 21st District, entered into the Congressional Record remarks relating to Karamu's plight. Included in those remarks was the following:

Mr. Speaker, unfortunately Karamu has not benefited financially from its efforts. As it begins its 75th year, this unique institution does so without the funds necessary to ensure its financial stability and future progress. While the theater is hailed throughout the country, community support has been lacking to provide the financial resources necessary to make Karamu a truly great arts center.

If you don't live in the Cleveland area, it doesn't matter. Across the nation, there are institutions of this type, undoubtedly with similar problems, that could use your involvement. The problems of lack of funding and support are somewhat universal, despite the excellent quality of leadership normally found in these institutions.

You Can't Teach Without Learning
Responsibility and Reward

"Please understand that sharing your knowledge and motivating others is beneficial and indispensable to your own personal and professional development"

One of the quickest and most rewarding ways to develop yourself is to share your talents and abilities with others. This does not mean doing for others what they can do for themselves.

It is wisely said that *"If you give a man a fish, you feed him for a day; but if you teach him to fish, you feed him for a lifetime."* Your challenge therefore would be to invoke the processes of teaching, leading, directing, encouraging, and otherwise causing others to move in the direction of self-fulfillment.

Consider that the world thirsts for knowledge and direction. Man has a natural curiosity for the world around him, a natural inclination to seek, and experiment, and improve. That is why we no longer make fire with stone, or transport water by mule.

Mental conditioning however causes many of us to limit our growth. We're afraid someone will laugh at us, or we were told that we couldn't do it. Remember that in any group you are a part of, it is likely that you know something, or have an idea that only you can share. If you don't bring your idea to the table, you will never know if it's any good.

Please understand that sharing your knowledge and motivating others is beneficial and indispensable to your own personal and professional development. I have never been in a teaching situation where I did not learn.

Questions from the student are the quickest and most effective way to cause reflection and re-evaluation by the teacher, and, in that regard, you will likely become wiser through feedback and further evaluation. You owe it to yourself and to your future to share what you have with the world. The world's slowest student will teach you, even if only the virtue of patience.

Another reason for teaching and helping others, is a moral obligation eloquently summarized by Ron Brown, former Chairman of the Democratic Party as he states,

> *One in three blacks still live in poverty. And, many more live in neighborhoods with poor schools, high crime, drug abuse, too few jobs, and too little hope. And, those of us who have made the most progress -- those of us who benefitted the most from the gains of recent years -- have the greatest responsibility to keep pressing for change.*

Mr. Brown further states that even in consideration for the hard work which has contributed to our success, *"we must never forget the broader social context in which our personal success has taken place. And, we must never stop working to extend that success to those whom it has yet to reach."*

Additionally, you should keep in mind that some young man or young woman in whom you created a thirst for knowledge, a desire to succeed, an example for living, might be the one God has chosen to find a cure for some dreaded disease. You might literally save your own life by turning a social liability into a savior of humanity.

Sharing Through Mentoring
Career Beginnings As An Example

"Mentor" is described in the dictionary as *"a wise and trusted advisor."* Suffice it to say that at the point someone in the position to know feels that you are qualified to become a mentor, you should go for it.

Mentorship creates for the mentor an obligation to another human being. If you assume that responsibility, hopefully you will be of such character that only your best will do. If that is the case, the student will assist you by keeping you on your toes.

In addition, I have experienced no greater feeling than knowing that I had some positive effect on another person who was seeking to better themselves, even if only to the extent that they knew I was available to listen.

You might ask *"Where do I start?"* Organizations such as Career Beginnings in Cleveland, Ohio, do an exceptional job by bringing together the philosophy of mentoring and the resources for organizing the mentoring process. Those resources include the students, the mentors, and the resources of education, business, and community. If your mind feeds exclusively from a diet of the 6 o'clock news, mentoring will likely introduce you to something much more digestible. It will introduce you to a sometimes underprivileged, often overlooked, and mostly underrated group of young people who have the capacity to achieve personal greatness with your help and involvement.

On the other hand, without your involvement, they have an equal or greater chance of becoming parasites in a society already overburdened by excesses of the unmotivated, the uneducated, the unsocialized, and the unconcerned.

- Section 7 -
In Conclusion

Where Do I Go From Here?
1994 And Beyond

Where Do You Go From Here?

Two Final Examples of Persistence

Quotables

Where Do I Go From Here?
1994 And Beyond

So much has occurred in my life during the twelve months preceding the deadline for this book that my life seems like a blur. Sometimes success can move so fast that you try not to blink for fear that you will miss something.

In October of 1993 I joined Toastmasters and the National Speakers Association, setting the stage for my meeting Dr. Robert Lawson. Dr. Lawson was instrumental in my getting this book published.

In May of 1994 I obtained my Bachelor's Degree in Business and Communications from Ohio's Capital University, graduating Magna Cum Laude, and being nominated for Student of The Year.

My graduation culminated four rewarding years in Capital's Adult Education program. The combination of small classes and individually focused learning made a difference. Bringing life's experiences into the classroom resulted in sharing what I had of value and learning what others had of value. If you have not obtained your Bachelor's degree because you doubt your ability to survive and grow in an academic environment, you should investigate adult education programs such as the one at Capital University. It could be the biggest single step you take toward success.

My graduation from Capital was not the end of my educational journey. Later in May, I participated in Dr. Lawson's seminar entitled *Destined For Greatness* and was thoroughly inspired. In early June I participated in Les Brown's workshop *Speaking For A Living*. Later that month I was honored to speak briefly at a church where Les was the featured speaker, and afterwards he and I talked at some length.

In early July, Les and I again met and discussed ways in which I could improve my marketability. I am extremely grateful for the time we have spent together. Later in July I signed the contract to complete *Success Is You*, realizing a vision that had been clouded by doubt for some time.

Those are just a few of the highlights, and to me they suggest that my time is here. Certainly there will be challenges and disappointments ahead, but that is what life is about. During the past year I have received training, mentoring and encouragement from the best and the brightest.

So now I must take responsibility for my future, as we all must. So that is where I go from here, onward and upward, being the best that I can be.

Where Do You Go From Here?

"Don't let what you don't have become your stumbling blocks, but let what you do have become your stepping stones. "

Perhaps the most difficult challenge I face in writing this book is how to end it. Realizing that the book may impact or fail to impact lives gives me a feeling of great responsibility. Those who write and speak for public consumption accept a heavy burden.

For like the great philosophers past and present, my conclusions and how they are interpreted *can* make a difference. I hope that what you have read will affect you in a positive way.

This book would not have been written had it not been for the encouragement of others who felt that I had something of value to write into the sands of time. The lack of the title *"Doctor"*, or not yet having a master's degree did not prevent me from writing this book. Don't let what you don't have become your stumbling block, but let what you do have become your stepping stone.

I have found out that in life, it's not what you are taught that matters, it's what you learn. I have found out that in life, it's not only what's in your head that matters, but also what's in your heart.

So what I do not yet have, or have not yet achieved, or did not adequately impart, cannot be used as your excuse not to succeed. You brought to the world a uniqueness that distinguishes you from all others. What I have failed to relate to you should not be construed as unnecessary for you to learn.

So from this time and place, where you go depends upon you. The torch has been passed. Go forth into the world and let your light shine, remembering always that -

Success Is You!

You

are an extension of a power greater than your own. You have been equipped with senses, the power of which has not been duplicated. Let me assure you that most of what you seek can be yours, if you will take action in accordance with that thought, and if you will believe that

SUCCESS IS YOU!

Henry Ford

Two Final Examples of Persistence

The Coca-Cola company sold only four hundred Cokes in its first year of business.

Dr. Seuss's first book was rejected by twenty-three publishers.

Quotables from *The O.E.C.U. Educator*
A Quarterly Newsletter of the Ohio Educational Credit Union

"To handle yourself, use your head, to handle others, use your heart."

"Feeling gratitude and not expressing it is like wrapping a present and not giving it."
- William Arthur Ward in *QUOTE*

"We make a living by what we get, but we make a life by what we give."
- Anonymous

"Life is under no obligation to give us what we expect."
- Margaret Mitchell

"Service to others is the rent I pay for my room here on earth."
- Muhammed Ali

"A happy person is not a person in a certain set of circumstances, but rather a person with a certain set of attitudes."
- Hugh Downes

Notes

1 *"Shoebox Lunch"* is a term heard many times during my youth. The lunch typically consisted of fried chicken, homemade cake, sandwiches and other foods that would not spoil on a long trip. They were packed to avoid having to stop when travelling through southern states where blacks were not welcome at restaurants. Usually a real shoe box was used because it protected the food from being crushed in tightly packed car trunks or tight passenger compartments. The shoe box was also compact enough to fit into cramped quarters.

2 *"It's too warm in the frying pan and too hot in the fire"* is a phrase meaning that you've got a problem no matter what action you take.

3 The public opinion poll referred to in Frankl's book was not named.

Works Cited

Bennis, Warren. *The Unconscious Conspiracy.* New York: AMACOM, A Division of American Management Association, 1976

Brown, Les. *Live Your Dreams.* New York: William Morrow and Company, 1992

Carnegie, Dale. *How to Develop Self-Confidence and Influence People by Public Speaking.* New York: Pocket Books, 1956

Ford, Henry. Workshop. *The Dream, Part II.* Detroit: August, 1992

Frankl, Dr. Viktor E. *Man's Search for Meaning.* New York: Simon & Schuster, 1963

Gould, Stephen Jay. *The Mismeasure of Man.* New York: W.W. Norton & Company, 1981

Johnson, Eric W. *Raising Children to Achieve.* New York: Walker Publishing, 1984

Kimbro, Dr. Dennis and Napoleon Hill. *Think and Grow Rich, A Black Choice.* New York: Ballantine Books, 1991

King, Rev. Dr. Martin Luther. Speech. *"I Have A Dream."* March On Washington. Washington, 22 Aug. 1963.

McClaney, Eula and Dr. La-Doris McClaney. *God, I Listened.* Beverly Hills, CA: Dr. La-Doris McClancy, 1989

Mish, Frederick C. *Webster's Ninth New Collegiate Dictionary.* 1990 ed. Unknown Author.

Professional Write Software. Software Publishing Corporation, 1990

Viscott, Dr. David. *Risking.* New York: Pocket Books of Simon & Schuster, 1977

Ziglar, Zig. *See You At The Top.* Gretna, Louisiana: Pelican Publishing, 1991

Index

About the Author

Henry Ford's unique combination of attitude, persistence and faith is reflected in his speeches, workshops and writings. At an age when many would have settled for boredom and complacency, he began a second career as a speaker and writer, defying aptitude test scores that indicated he should do neither.

In the twelve months preceding the release of _Success Is You_, Henry became a member of Toastmasters, the Ohio Speakers Forum and the National Speakers Association. He actively participated in workshops and other training, earning two Toastmaster awards. In May, 1994, Henry graduated from the Adult Degree program at Ohio's Capital University, where he frequently participates in student orientation sessions.

As a member of a race which historically has been incorrectly judged as inferior, Henry reveals the fallacy of those beliefs. He destroys the myth of inferiority as he exposes the principles of success to diverse audiences.

Dr. Jack Hearns, former school superintendent writes _"Your speech should be published and made standard reading for teachers and PTA units."_ The _Twinsburg Sun Times_ reported in its May 27, 1993 issue, _"His voice is deep and velvety, his style methodical and deliberate. His strong, clear delivery emphasizes his faith in his message."_ Pastor Rev. Walter L. Boykins states _"I want our speaker to know that the pulpit is open at Grace Missionary."_ Internationally recognized speaker Les Brown wrote simply _"You have the Gift."_

For further information, write or call:

Henry Ford
FORD & Associates
P.O. Box 393
Twinsburg, OH 44087-0393

(216) 425-8776   or   (216) 348-4612 - 24 Hour Voice Mail

To contact the author, write:
Henry E. Ford
P.O. Box 393
Twinsburg, OH 44087-0393

Order Form

YES! I want _____ copies of *Success is You* at $16.95 each, plus
$3.50 shipping and handling per book. ISBN # 0-7872-0232-0.

Call 1-800-228-0810 to order by telephone or Fax 1-800-772-9165.
Prepayment is required.

☐Check
enclosed
☐ Charge my
    account:

☐ Master Card   ☐ American Express   ☐ Visa

MC Bank #|_|_|_|_|_| Exp. Date ___/___/___

Account #|_|_|_|_|_|_|_|_|_|_|_|_|_|_|_|_|_|_|_|_|_|_|_|_|

Signature_____
(required for all charges)

Name_____

Phone (_____)_____

Address_____

_____

City/State/Zip_____

Please make check payable to:

Kendall/Hunt Publishing Company
4050 Westmark Drive
Dubuque, Iowa 52004-1840